P9-EMR-769

The
TRUE
GERMAN

The
TRUE
GERMAN

THE DIARY OF A
WORLD WAR II
MILITARY JUDGE

WERNER OTTO MÜLLER-HILL

INTRODUCTION BY
BENJAMIN CARTER HETT

TRANSLATED AND WITH ADDITIONAL
EDITING BY JEFFERSON CHASE

palgrave
macmillan

THE TRUE GERMAN
Copyright © Michalon Editeur, 2011.
English-language translation copyright © 2013 by Jefferson Chase.
All rights reserved.

First published in France as *Journal de Guerre d'un Juge Militaire Allemande 1944–1945* by Michalon Editeur.

First published in English in 2013 by PALGRAVE MACMILLAN® in the US—a division of St. Martin's Press LLC, 175 Fifth Avenue, New York, NY 10010.

Where this book is distributed in the UK, Europe and the rest of the world, this is by Palgrave Macmillan, a division of Macmillan Publishers Limited, registered in England, company number 785998, of Houndmills, Basingstoke, Hampshire RG21 6XS.

Palgrave Macmillan is the global academic imprint of the above companies and has companies and representatives throughout the world.

Palgrave® and Macmillan® are registered trademarks in the United States, the United Kingdom, Europe and other countries.

All photographs and images come from the original diary or the Müller-Hill family.

ISBN-13: 978-1-137-27854-8

Library of Congress Cataloging-in-Publication Data is available from the Library of Congress.

A catalogue record of the book is available from the British Library.

Design by Letra Libre, Inc.

First edition: September 2013

10 9 8 7 6 5 4 3 2 1

Printed in the United States of America

CONTENTS

A NOTE ON THE TEXT

Werner Otto Müller-Hill's diary is published with the kind permission of his son Benno Müller-Hill. Born in 1933, he can be seen at the age of four in the family photos in this volume. Not only is Benno Müller-Hill one of Germany's leading biochemists and geneticists, but he has also made important contributions to the field of bioethics, in particular on the subject of the natural sciences under National Socialism. He lives in Cologne.

TRANSLATOR'S NOTE

As I discovered while working on the diary kept by Werner Otto Müller-Hill in the final years of World War II, there is a big difference between translating a work of history and translating a historical source. With the former, the translator tries to remedy weak spots in the original and adapt the work so that it can have maximum impact on its new foreign audience. With the latter, the emphasis must be on staying close the original so the past can speak as directly—not as elegantly—as possible to the audience. In this spirit, my translation of Müller-Hill's diary is very much "warts and all."

Müller-Hill was a judge, not a professional author. Although he writes fairly clear prose for the time, his style reflects his era and is a bit long-winded, hair-splitting, even prissy by today's standards. I've made no effort to smooth over stylistic infelicities, cut out repetitions, or tighten up arguments. If we take Müller-Hill at his word, he kept this diary as record of what he thought and felt for his son, not because he knew he was going to be published someday, and today's readers should keep that in mind.

Nor should we expect the opinions he expresses in these pages to conform to our notions of consistency or acceptability. Müller-Hill realized the Third Reich was waging an ignominious and unwinnable war and exercised leniency as a judge in cases that a fervent ideologue would have treated harshly. However, his opposition to Nazism was born of his German patriotism. First and foremost, he despised Hitler and his henchmen for what they did to Germany, not for what they did to Europe or Europe's Jews. He acknowledged that Germans had perpetrated an abominable injustice upon Jews without expressing the sort of empathy we would now demand for people treated so gruesomely. At one point he even raged at the thought of (presumably American) "Negroes" destroying the venerable, "cultured" city of Strasbourg. I haven't sought to tone down such passages or make them acceptable to contemporary sensibilities. What's striking about the historical figure and document we encounter here are precisely such contradictions. Müller-Hill was no Oskar Schindler or Claus von Stauffenberg, but I suspect that if we could ask even these undeniably courageous men what they thought about Jews, people of color, or the working classes today, we also would find some of their answers shocking.

One running theme I found interesting and somewhat unexpected is the importance placed on regional identity.

Müller-Hill was a native and lifelong resident of Freiburg. Residents of the southwestern corner of Germany, where the country comes together with France and Switzerland, speak in strong dialect and pride themselves on Alemannic customs and an Alemannic mindset not found anywhere else in Germany. Together with rest of Alsace-Lorraine, the city of Strasbourg, where Müller-Hill was stationed as he began his diary, had been part of Germany from 1870 to 1918. Freiburg and Strasbourg are only 53 miles from one another. Thus, it's perhaps understandable that Müller-Hill did not see himself as an occupying foreign invader. His sense of local Alemannic identity also led him to associate many aspects of Nazism he most detested with Prussia in northeastern Germany—which runs contrary to the historical facts that the Nazi movement began in southern Germany and initially had trouble bringing some segments of the Prussian bureaucracy into line. Again I felt it was my task as a translator to let Müller-Hill speak for himself, even when I thought he was wrong.

Unlike a work of history, a historical document doesn't have to be right to be worth reading. In terms of perspicacity and analytic insight, Müller-Hill's diary may not compare very well to those written by Victor Klemperer. Klemperer, though, was an academic forced into an extreme outsider position that encouraged an extraordinary clarity of vision. Müller-Hill was an upper-middle-class member of the social mainstream who internally rejected the positions of a government he came to abhor, and refused, where he felt he could, to put them into practice. Much has been written on the phenomenon of "inner emigration" in Nazi Germany and other dictatorships and totalitarian systems. Müller-Hill's diary is an example of this idea, which is slippery and self-serving. After World War II, it was easy for Germans to claim that, in their heart of hearts, they'd opposed the Hitler regime. Such assertions could neither be proven nor disproven. Müller-Hill put his highly critical opinions down on paper, and for that reason alone, what he wrote merits attention.

Finally, I was also struck by the fact that, although Müller-Hill felt nothing but contempt for his Nazi superiors and performed his job contrary to the spirit of his instructions, he still tried to keep functioning within the system for as long as he could. One of the most difficult things to understand about Germans' behavior in the final weeks and months of World War II is why so many carried on even though the battle was obviously lost, and continued resistance meant courting even greater disaster. It is very difficult to wish for or choose defeat for one's own kind. Many Americans, for instance, opposed the Second Iraq War. But how many of them rooted for the United States to fail? Müller-Hill's diary is shot through with a similar ambiguity, perhaps contradiction. By not resolving the inconsistencies, I've tried to give readers access not just to a bygone time, but to a fundamentally human disconnect between attitudes and behavior. Works of history are supposed to be logical, consistent and thoroughly reasoned out. Historical material—our most direct immediate source of how people acted in the past—is anything but those things.

Jefferson Chase
Berlin, April 2013

INTRODUCTION

BENJAMIN CARTER HETT

In July 1944 the German General Ferdinand Schörner, commanding Army Group North in the Baltic (whose soldiers were by then in a desperate situation, surrounded and cut off from any retreat to Germany by the massive Soviet summer offensive) paid a call on one of his senior military judges. Schörner opened the conversation by asking the judge "How many men have you hanged so far?" Rather taken aback, the judge replied, "The Military Penal Code provides only for executions by firing squad, Herr General."

"So that means that you are still only shooting your men," said Schörner, with evident disgust. He proceeded to explain what he expected military judges under his command to do. "We hang the men, and not just at any out-of-the-way place where no one will see them, but at the front control centers, at the hostels for soldiers on leave, at train stations. They stay hanging there for three days, until they stink. Whoever hasn't seen them yet, smells them. That strengthens the men. I am telling you." Schörner finished with menace, "My judges must learn how to be unjust."[1]

Schörner was a demonstrable psychopath, but his outburst nonetheless captures the spirit of German military "justice" in World War II. While German military courts in World War I had sentenced 48 soldiers to death, their successors between 1933 and 1945 condemned at least 20,000, and by some accounts as many as 33,000 or more soldiers, prisoners of war, and civilians subject to military justice to the same fate. The offenses ranged from those recognized by any army—desertion or attacks on a superior officer—to those with a distinctively Nazi flavor—"corrosion of military morale" or "military treason." By the last phase of the war, drumhead courts were executing soldiers in huge numbers on the slightest pretext and with hardly a gesture in the direction of normal legal procedures.[2]

Nor was extraordinary harshness toward their own troops the only stain on the record of Nazi military jurists. It was military lawyers, for instance, who in the run-up to the German invasion of the Soviet Union in 1941 drafted the infamous Commissar Order calling for mass shootings behind the lines—which historians recognize as a major step on the path to the Holocaust. They also prepared the Order for Conduct toward Russian Prisoners of War which cleared the way for the Germans to murder some 3 million Soviet captives, mostly through enclosing them behind barbed wire and leaving them to starve to death. In the words of one historian, the work of German military lawyers in World War

II amounted to nothing less than the building of a "facade behind which mass murder could appear as legal."[3]

Yet here, in the wartime diary of German military judge Werner Otto Müller-Hill, we have the remarkable record of a man who, from inside this murderous system, never sentenced a man to death and saw it as his mission to protect and defend the soldiers who came before him. More than that: Müller-Hill was an implacable opponent of the Nazis, who managed to avoid becoming a member of the Nazi Party or any of its affiliated organizations. He was a shrewd critic and analyst of Nazi propaganda, an unusually talented forecaster of coming political developments, and— not least—a thoughtful commentator on his own people and their response to the catastrophic events of World War II. At a time in which historians and general readers alike are as fascinated as ever by questions of what Germans in the Third Reich knew and when they knew it, what they believed and what they did, the appearance of this diary is both timely and important.

Müller-Hill was born in Freiburg im Breisgau, on the edge of the Black Forest, in 1885, the son of an engineer father and a pianist and singer mother. He received an education typical of upper-middle class young men in the Kaiser's Germany, starting with studies at a *Gymnasium,* an academic high school which delivered a thorough and rigorous, if unimaginative, classical education, and going on between 1907 and 1912 to study law at the University of Freiburg. He was already practicing as a lawyer in Freiburg by 1913. The only unusual element of this education and training is Müller-Hill's lack of mobility: German students of that time would typically move around and study at two or three different universities. Müller-Hill was wedded to his native Baden.

He served as a military judge even during the First World War, before returning in 1919 to private legal practice. At the beginning of 1940 he was again called up for service as a military judge. For most of the war he stayed not far from home—from February 1942 until October 1944 he was on the staff of the 158th (later renamed the 405th) replacement division in Stasbourg, until the worsening military situation forced the divisional staff to relocate to Oberkirch in southern Baden and then later to Tübingen.

At the end of the war he was already 60 years old, but he returned to his legal career, serving in the late 1940s as a senior prosecutor (*Oberstaatsanwalt*) in the small town of Offenburg in Baden. In 1950 he retired, but his retirement was long; Müller-Hill died in 1977.[4]

GERMAN MILITARY JUDGES IN WORLD WAR II

still administered the old Military Penal Code of 1872 and the Code of Military Judicial Procedure of 1898—but, as in other areas of Nazi law, with substantial amendments introduced piecemeal by decree, particularly through the Special Wartime Penal Decree (*Kriegssonderstrafrechtsverordnung,* KSSVO) and the Code of Wartime Criminal Procedure (*Kriegsstrafverfahrensordnung,* KStVO) both promulgated in August 1938 and repeatedly amended. The point of these laws was to avoid what the Nazis saw as the failure of German military courts in World War I to prevent erosion of morale and eventual defeat. Nazi military law, therefore, specified both harsh penalties and a speedy procedure, with few rights for defendants.

The nature of the courts in which Müller-Hill worked was outlined in the KStVO. A military court had three judges, of which only one was a trained lawyer, while the others were to be regular soldiers—if possible, one of them of the rank of the accused, the other a senior officer. To ensure that courts imposed the harsh justice the high command and the regime wanted, everything that a court did, from the assignment of lawyers and judges to the decisions they reached, was subject to the control and approval of the commanding officer of the formation the court served, usually the divisional commanding officer; in his judicial capacity the commanding officer was designated the "lord of the court" (*Gerichtsherr*). Judges often played different roles in different proceedings. The same official could be deployed as an investigator or prosecutor as well as in the role of a judge, depending on the flow of business and the whim of the lord of the court (hints in Müller-Hill's diary suggest that he also played these various different roles). Defendants had the right to a defense counsel only in cases where the death penalty was possible, but the code allowed even this right to be neglected if the "war of movement" so required. Research has suggested that in fact defendants seldom had the benefit of a defense, even where they theoretically had a right to one.[5]

Of cases that resulted in a death penalty, by far the most common was deserting the colors, with corrosion of military morale a distant second. "Corrosion" could include such actions as inflicting a wound on oneself; seeking to undermine discipline; encouraging others to disobey orders, to desert, or to attack a superior officer; or refusing military service. A wide range of other and more minor offenses could also bring a soldier up on charges, of which the most common was the theft of packages or supplies. One of the leading scholars in this area has estimated that as many as 2.5 million German military personnel—of the 16 million mobilized for the war—had some experience of a case in a military court. And of these, perhaps 50 to 60 percent were convicted.[6]

MÜLLER-HILL'S DIARY IS ESPECIALLY IMportant as a sign of what it was possible for an intelligent citizen to know, or at least to figure out, in Hitler's Germany. He knew full well that keeping such a diary was dangerous: if it were discovered, he wrote in the document itself, "It would mean death. I'd be dismissed from my post and handed over as a civilian to the Gestapo [the secret police] for reeducation." Why did he run this risk? No historical source is ever self-interpreting, and we can only speculate about his motives. It is striking that the diary begins in March 1944, by which time it was clear to any rational observer that Germany would lose the war. No doubt, like many diarists, Müller-Hill wanted to "bear witness" to great events. Perhaps his abundant critical faculties demanded an outlet otherwise unobtainable in Nazi Germany. But it is also possible, as Wolfram Wette writes in the introduction to the German edition, that he wanted to create a document for his own exculpation after a clearly foreseeable Allied victory. Though a critic of the regime, he was also still its uniformed servant, and he was more than far-sighted enough to understand the legal danger he might be in after defeat.[7]

In the early days of historical research on Nazi Germany, most scholars assumed that Hitler's Reich had been a monolithic and "totalitarian" society, in which, through a combination of brutal terror and brilliantly orchestrated propaganda, Germans were reduced to the status of a helpless and unthinking mass. Had this been true it would be entirely idle to speak of "public opinion" in Nazi Germany. But research over the past couple of decades has pointed up many limitations in this model of Nazi society, and many old beliefs about the Third Reich have been overturned. Joseph Goebbels, the Nazi minister of "Public Enlightenment and Propaganda," was by no means the sinister master of mass deception that he claimed to be and that many historians, themselves perhaps hypnotized by Goebbels's extensive and important diaries, had earlier taken him for. Perhaps he did not need to be: the regime in any case enjoyed genuine, strong, and unforced support from a majority—though by no means all—of its citizens. But there were real limits on how far the Nazis could impose their views on Germans. They succeeded in winning popular compliance where their message went with the grain of German beliefs, whether in matters of religion, national defense, economic management, or sexuality, to take a few examples.[8]

This newer and more complex understanding of the Third Reich naturally casts an important, and disturbing, light on Germans' compliance with (or at least nonresistance to) the regime's worst crimes. Virtually obsessed with the fear of a wartime breakdown of morale on the home front, the regime was sensitive to public opinion and often willing to cater to it. In summer 1941 public sermons preached by Klemens von Galen, the Catholic bishop of Münster, forced the regime to scale back its "Euthanasia" program of the murder of Germans with physical and mental handicaps. In February and March 1943, when the Nazis set out to deport Jewish men married to non-Jewish women from Berlin to the death camps in Poland, mass protests by the "German" wives and other women in Berlin's Rosenstrasse forced the regime to back down and let the men go, and even to rescue a few who had already been sent east. But wider protests against the treatment of Jews were conspicuous by their rarity; institutions like universities, professional associations, government ministries, and churches (as distinct from a few individuals such as Bishop Galen or the theologian Dietrich Bonhoeffer) did not protest at all.[9]

Of course, individual human beings, as much as the societies they inhabit, are complex and will almost always evade easy generalizations. The Germany that the Nazis took over in 1933 was a sophisticated modern society, with long-standing and often bitter divisions between classes, political parties, confessions, and regions. The Nazis succeeded in gaining substantial support from different kinds of Germans to different degrees; their propaganda ("one people, one state, one leader") could paper over the real divisions among Germans, but could not make these divisions disappear. Well-heeled travelers tried to avoid the resorts frequented by the down-market, packaged "Strength through Joy" tours; Bavarians remained suspicious of Prussians, Catholics of Protestants, workers of bosses. What is true of society as a whole is also true of individuals: opinions did not always line up to meet our expectations. In June 1941 a mother worried over a son missing since the sinking of the battleship *Bismarck* greeted the news of the German invasion of the Soviet Union with the lament "our youth is bleeding! The young men fall, the girls don't get men, the children remain unborn, always the same, terrible bill of war." She yearned only for peace and her son's safe return, and complained bitterly that Germany had "carelessly" let him die. But this didn't keep her from noting that "no one doubted" that Germany would defeat the Soviet Union, and that in ordering this invasion "the Führer has once again absolutely done the right thing." Bishop Galen himself was an ardent German nationalist with far-right political views. Much the same was true of many of the men whose repeated attempts to kill Hitler culminated in the famous "Valkyrie" plot.[10]

It seems safe to say that most Germans most of the time accepted most of the regime's broader claims. Letters and diaries from 1941, for instance, from soldiers and civilians alike, reveal a striking readiness to believe that Germany's war against the Soviet Union was "preventive," that the German attack had narrowly averted a catastrophic Soviet assault on Germany. Research on the last phase of the war shows many Germans still invested improbable hopes in "wonder weapons," a fatal split between the Allies, or in the Ardennes counteroffensive of Christmas 1944 (the Battle of the Bulge)—indeed Müller-Hill's diary also records his colleagues' misplaced faith in these official claims.[11]

Research on what the German people knew is most sensitive, but most important, when it comes to the Holocaust. Historical research has dispatched the common postwar apologetic claim that the mass murder of Jews had been a terrible secret of which Germans only learned when Hitler was defeated. But of course there are different kinds and degrees of "knowing." Considerable evidence points to widespread German civilian knowledge of the "Holocaust by bullets"—the mass shootings of Jews by the SS *Einsatzgruppen* (special task forces) in Poland and the Soviet Union in 1941 and 1942. Knowledge of the "Holocaust by gas"—mass murder by poison gas in camps built for the purpose, like Treblinka or Sobibor—was more limited and probably more widespread in eastern Germany than in the west. But perhaps the most important point is that, in the words of historian Ian Kershaw, "the road to Auschwitz was built by hate, but paved with indifference." Most Germans simply did not care very much one way or another what was happening to the Jews; between 1942 and 1944, when most of the killings took place, Germans were dealing with a steadily worsening war, mounting battlefield casualties, and escalating aerial bombardment of their cities. As Kershaw writes, the fate of a small and unpopular minority simply ranked well down their list of priorities. Historians broadly agree that the regime's grip on its people, its claims on their obedience, and the brutality of its repressive measures all moved to their peak precisely as the regime itself neared collapse.[12]

Against this background, Müller-Hill's intelligence and independence of mind stand out as truly remarkable. From the evidence of this diary, Müller-Hill had little privileged access to high-level information sources. He even claimed—and there is no reason not to believe him—that he stayed away from the one non-German information source to which so many Germans had ready, albeit covert, access: foreign news broadcasts, especially those of the BBC. Müller-Hill thought this particular indulgence was "too dangerous." He stuck to the source to which any German had (legal) access: the Nazis' own tightly controlled media. Yet from the regime's radio and newspapers he was able, time and again, to draw conclusions remarkable for their acuity and prescience. He had nothing but contempt for a senior officer who claimed that "only a person who listened to foreign radio could be unsure of our victory." If the man really meant what he said, wrote Müller-Hill, it revealed only "how hollow his head is." "My thinking apparatus is still working normally," he added, "without being externally 'steered.'"[13]

He understood the shape of the war that Germany had fought and was fighting. The March 1939 invasion of Bohemia and Moravia had been more "provocative" than Hitler's bid for Danzig in the drive to war—although he also knew that the outbreak of war in 1939 had not really been over Danzig and the Polish Corridor, but rather about "recalibrating the relations of power in Europe." In April 1944 he wrote "I'm one of the 'pessimists' who think that the die was cast when we failed to defeat Russia and they counterattacked." Here he seems to be referring to the Soviet counterattack before Moscow in December 1941, which indeed many subsequent military historians (and some German generals at the time) viewed as the real turning point of the war.[14]

At almost all times Müller-Hill had a shrewd appreciation for what was coming. Already in April 1944 he understood that the scale and ferocity of Nazi repression would "rule out a revolutionary collapse in Germany." Defeat would then inevitably mean that Germany would be completely occupied after the whole of the country had been fought over, an "unavoidable fate": "We are rushing headlong toward the most extreme form of defeat." Always skeptical of Nazi claims, he did not expect any salvation from Hitler's promised V weapons. In December 1944 radio broadcasts carried the first reports of the German offensive in the Ardennes, which lead to the Battle of the Bulge. His fellow officers expected victory; Müller-Hill could only think of parallels to the spring offensive of 1918, another desperate German attempt to ward off near-certain defeat. Showing his strong sense of reality, he wondered, "Where are we going to get fuel for our tanks? And warplanes?" Of course he was right, and when the failure of the offensive became clear, he wrote that the war would end in three or six months—a good estimate, as in fact it was to be a little over four. He understood long before the end of the war, and far better than the Allies did for several more years, that efforts to "denazify" Germany would not work well: "The public apparatus of the state is so entwined with the party that it's impossible to imagine how the state can be repositioned under an occupation if the occupiers exclude everyone who was active in the movement or a member of the party."[15]

On the other hand, perhaps surprisingly—or perhaps not—he remained closemouthed about his own judicial work. To be sure, he wrote that he was "considered far too lenient," and that "my mildness as a judge is probably the reason I wasn't promoted." He considered it his job to protect soldiers who had "slipped up" and to prevent "immoral, humiliating punishments." This is entirely plausible, although he provided no specifics. At the same time he was certainly not ideologically opposed to the basic task he had to perform and he had much of the outlook that we would expect from a conservative and patriotic German of the mid-twentieth cetury. In April 1944, for instance, he wrote about cases of corrosion of morale which occupied the courts a good deal in the closing phase of the Nazi regime. The idea for this offense came out of the regime's desire to combat "the literal sort" of corrosion "as practiced by the Independent Social Democrats in 1917 and 1918," and thus to avoid "a so-called stab in the back from within"—whereby Müller-Hill seemed to accept that German socialists really did "corrode" morale at the end of World War I and that there was validity to the "stab in the back" legend that Germany lost that war because of internal revolt rather than military defeat (although in other places he showed his skepticism of this legend). This "stab in the back" idea was widely accepted by conservative Germans in the interwar years, and it helped to fuel radical nationalist resentments like those expressed by the Nazis. In February 1945 he noted that many of his cases were being suspended, so that "practically the only rulings we have to make are on the crassest forms of desertion and deadly attacks on a superior"—clearly cases in which he felt no compunction about reaching severe verdicts.[16]

He knew—he had to know—how brutal German military justice was, especially in the last phase of the war. "Our 'harshest' judge," he wrote at the end of March 1945, "had been appointed to head the drumhead court in Tübingen and is expected to set heads rolling for final victory!" Perhaps oddly, he added that this judge was not to be envied: "The job is unpleasant even for someone who is indeed too harsh and without any human feelings." This line hints at a good deal of personal experience that Müller-Hill was not keen to share, even with his diary. He recognized that in their savage zeal to impose punishment German courts exceeded the limits the law prescribed. The essence of corrosion of morale

was that it had to be demonstrated in a public act or statement, but the courts were increasingly prosecuting private
expressions, and thus judicial reasoning "is increasingly divorced from the initial legal logic that created this category
of crime."[17]

We should not expect Müller-Hill to be what he was not:
a citizen of a democracy of the early twenty-first century,
with all the views that that would entail. He was a conservative and patriotic German, a military officer in wartime. He
did not want his country to lose. "It would be appropriate,"
he wrote, "to *demand* every form of sacrifice from the border regions, even their total destruction," if doing so would
halt the Allied advance and end the war. He was only too
skeptical to think such a plan would work. He had a patriot's high regard for the performance of German soldiers.
In October 1944 he wrote that "what our troops are achieving right now in the west and the east exceeds everything
they've done previously. Our operative reserves are dwindling as our enemies' armies are growing, and still we are
never overrun." A few days later he wrote that the German
army's fighting strength "seems truly miraculous," and Germans' military performance and willingness to make sacri-
fices entitled them—"the bruised and bleeding populace, not
the Nazis"—to a "more honorable peace."[18]

Yet sometimes Müller-Hill vented his exasperation with
the mass of his countrymen who did not possess his acuity. The German people were "the most naive mass ever to
populate a continent." There were still many who said "that

the Führer *must* have something up his sleeve" or he would not still dare to predict final victory. "God knows," wrote Müller-Hill, "our leaders have picked the right people to match their brand of politics."[19]

Readers will certainly come to Müller-Hill's diary wondering what he knew and what he had to say about the Holocaust, and I do not want to steal his thunder. Suffice it say that he knew a lot; the text offers a highly instructive guide to what it was possible for a German to know in 1944, as well as grounds for important inferences about how widespread this knowledge was and what kind of attitudes Germans had to the persecution of Jews.

The book is also a striking record of what Germans experienced in the last phase of the war. Müller-Hill's wife and son remained in Freiburg im Breisgau. In late November 1944 Freiburg was bombed by the Royal Air Force and heavily damaged. Müller-Hill's family survived, but their house was destroyed. He got "bomb leave" to go and see to their relocation, and a gap in the diary from November 22 to December 15 suggests the strain he was under. In March 1945, the day he heard the Americans had crossed the Rhine at Remagen, he gave voice to despair: "We three—bombed out, impoverished, homeless, and without bed, kitchen, and apartment—are just a small part of the millions of people who are doing equally badly and whose fate doesn't move our genius of a Führer in the slightest." A higher power, he thought, was demanding this "test" because "once destruction has come to Germany, the idea of National Socialism will be eradicated once and for all" and the military in particular would be "utterly uprooted and discarded."[20]

IN FACT THE NAZIS' MILITARY JUSTICE SYStem, like their regime as a whole, cast a long shadow over postwar Germany. On one level this was suprising: unlike the perpetrators of the Holocaust or most other Nazi crimes, whose victims were either German minorities or foreigners, the judges who imposed such a horrifying number of death sentences targeted men from the very heart of German society. Indeed, when Ferdinand Schörner returned to Germany from Soviet captivity in 1955, he was greeted by scathing newspaper editorials, and tough young men with vengeance on their minds were waiting for his train in Munich.[21]

Yet it took decades for awareness of the atrocities of Nazi military judges to penetrate the general public consciousness and even the work of historians. In part, military judges benefited from the legend of the "clean *Wehrmacht*" zealously circulated by surviving senior commanders like Franz Halder and Erich von Manstein—the idea that the armed forces (*Wehrmacht*) had fought an honorable war in defense of their country, like soldiers in all times and places, while the guilt for Nazi crimes rested solely on Nazis organizations like the SS and the Gestapo. This legend has only been thoroughly dispatched in comparatively recent years. But in part the former military judges took up important positions in postwar West German society, and their collective institutional clout also shielded them from scrutiny. Already by 1948 nearly 10 percent of appellate judges in the British zone of occupation were former military judges, and as many as 80 to 90 percent of trial judges were former Nazi Party members, of which again a considerable number had been military judges. One of the most eminent and influential scholars of German criminal law and its history in the postwar years, Eberhard Schmidt, was a former military judge (who during the war had enthusiastically advocated that the civilian justice system should adopt the draconian procedures of military courts); and so, until a scandal over his wartime past forced him from office, was Hans Filbinger, governor of the state of Baden-Württemberg from 1966 to 1978. Filbinger defended himself from a storm of criticism over miserably unjust death sentences he had imposed with the words "what was legal then can't be an injustice now." This was a view which military judges had consistently held, and imposed on their country, ever since the end of the war. In 1956 the West German Supreme Court found that the April 1945 verdicts sentencing the resistance fighters Admiral Wilhelm Canaris and General Hans Oster to death had been "in accordance with the law," because one could not deny the National Socialist regime its own "right of self-preservation." The author of this verdict was a former military judge.[22]

It is thus all the more remarkable that Werner Otto Müller-Hill saw this engine of terror for what it was, even as he served it. His clear-sightedness, independence, and humanity, can now, in this volume, find their belated honor.

JOURNAL ENTRIES

MARCH 28, 1944–
JUNE 7, 1945

"You could see it coming, but it still shakes you to the core."

—Journal entry, April 12, 1944

My decision to begin a diary on the day after my 59th birth-day, which like the four preceding ones, I "celebrated" in uniform, was prompted by a book that I received yesterday as a gift. It's Bouhler's *Napoleon,* a book that does justice to one of the great pioneers of power politics, a man who—despite many seeming similarities—is not comparable to his successor, this creature possessed by a demon.[1] The former was a far greater figure in terms of human stature and qualities, with nothing of the intolerable narrow-mindedness and small-spiritedness that is National Socialism. The book bows down before France and yet is written with vested German interests in mind. Bouhler fancies that he has uncovered the reasons that led to this titan's fall. And yet when he follows Stendhal in asserting that Napoleon was brought down "firstly by a love of mediocre people that he had maintained since his coronation and secondly by the merging of the job of an emperor with that of a general," it's impossible not to make comparisons—the difference being that H.'s military and political leadership were both disastrous.[2]

The most obvious similarity is that in both cases the impossibility of invading England led to a campaign against

Russia and that was the beginning of the end. Yet here, too, there is a fundamental difference. In the case of Napoleon, a large-scale invading army shattered into smithereens. With Hitler, the army has remained intact despite all the setbacks but at the cost of plunging half a generation of German youth into the maelstrom of all-consuming struggle. The center of the eastern front is still intact, even though the Russian has penetrated Romania.[3] And it's anyone's guess how long the center, lacking virility and barely able to supply itself, can stay on its feet.

The Müller-Hill family in the mid-1930s

All of this appears so utterly hopeless to a thinking mind that you can only scratch your head when comrades in your unit speak privately of the certainty and not merely the possibility of victory. Such people talk about a quasi-mythical "weapon of retribution" that will be deployed any day now.[4] They fantasize about a destruction of the south coast of England, in which troops that may be massing there will be "pulverized," so that we and not our enemies will be the ones planning a military landing.

Such people are living in a dreamland from which I fear they will be terribly awakened. I, on the contrary, am of the opinion that a military catastrophe will be unavoidable if the enemy launches a large-scale invasion. And our enemies have more than enough time to prepare one—no matter how eloquently General [Kurt] Dittmar may have spoken today about our defensive triumphs in Cassino.[5]

It is impossible, of course, to broach the things I entrust to this journal in conversation without being completely certain that any given discussion partner shares my opinions—although I can indeed say that about several comrades whose names I will refrain from mentioning. Perhaps, if I should survive the war, it will be of some interest to my son to read the frank assessments of a military judge in what I am convinced is the final phase of the war.

It's impossible to estimate today how long this phase will last. Recently Dr. [Joseph] Goebbels wrote about the difficulty of making hard-and-fast predictions—before going on, for Hitler's sake—to offer a general prognosis of victory. I'm even less able to read the future than he is. *My* prognosis is very simple: the war will last as long as *we* hold out.[6] As the situation stands, it is unthinkable that our enemies, with their vast superiority in men and matériel, might falter before we do. That would take a miracle and would presuppose that we don't capitulate, that the war will go on for so long that we are occupied by enemy forces after a series of individual defeats in the east and the west. An invasion will come sooner or later. Should our enemies not try to invade us, or should that invasion fail, it is difficult to envision how the war will end. It could take years until we capitulate—from sheer exhaustion.

Strasbourg
March 29, 1944

Nikolayevsk-on-Amur, too, has fallen. The route to Odessa over the Bug River seems to still be partially open. But will we try to hold our ground, with the Russian barreling down the Prut River and perhaps soon reaching Yasny? How will it be possible to supply this army? What a grim situation for the Southern Army. The papers are full of articles about Cassino to divert attention from southeastern front. Around ten days ago, a military correspondent (perhaps the multitalented Dittmar himself) wrote that the Russians' concentration of strength was not great enough for them to have any hope of crossing the Bug. And where are they today?

We need to be clear that these Russian victories are by no means miracles, even if we do have a skilled and decisive military leadership. Since July 1943, we have been exhausting poorly regenerated divisions, while the Russian can always throw new divisions into battle. It's more of a miracle that the Russian hasn't yet *completely* broken through our lines.

The Russian can shore up weak spots wherever he wants. We don't have this capacity. The tissue of our divisions is simply too thin to hold up everywhere. A little while ago, the local newspaper—unmentionably poorly edited, but where isn't that the case?—made a charming blunder of which Dr. Goebbels would surely have been quite critical. On page one, we read the usual statement about how England only declared war to prevent Danzig from becoming German.[7] On page three, there was a pompous speech by the local gauleiter, claiming that we had a right to Eastern European territory denied to us by the democracies.[8] It could hardly have been any clearer what we really want: the Ukraine, the Kuban region of southern Russia, and perhaps more. After all, you only realize how hungry you are after you've started to eat.

I remember well conversations I heard as a member of the Sixth Corps back when we invaded Russia. People were talking about three months. Field Marshal Walther von Brauchitsch supposedly said something similar to his generals shortly before June 22, 1941.[9] That only shows that he himself was as blind as his supreme commander.

It's also clear that we were hoping another Russian revolution would break out after the first few setbacks. *That's* how blind we were, but it's no accident. As the clever Count [Hermann] Keyserling convincingly noted in his *Spectrum of Europe,* we are the only Europeans who live as introverted thinkers in a world of ideas.[10] That's why K. calls us "windowless monads."

Our foreign policy, insofar as one can use the word "policy" in conjunction with someone as foolhardy as H., must be understood as part of this phenomenon. We made pretty damn daring gambits in the Rhineland, Austria, and Sudetenland,[11] all of which threatened the states hostile to us. Then we barbarically forced the issue on the Jewish question and cleverly earned ourselves the enmity of Jews all over the world. It was a miracle that the coup of [reoccupying the Rhineland in] March 1936 succeeded.[12] Jews would have surely welcomed a defeat for Hitler and one can't blame them. We only had 18 to 20 divisions back then. They would have been obliterated if France, the Czechs, and possibly Poland had attacked. *Had* they done so, millions of people would not have bled to death on the eastern front! But as things were, France was too content as a state to wage war, especially as England was applying the brakes.[13] Moreover, our demands back then were relatively moderate.[14] But this success made Hitler bolder in his tightrope walk on the cliff's edge of war, which England and France could not bring themselves to wage for three years.[15]

Our propaganda is very adroit in interpreting the fact that it was our claim to Danzig and the [Polish] Corridor which touched off the war, even though our invasion of Czech territory was far more provocative. And this propaganda has clouded the minds of the German to the extent that he can no longer see the lengthy chain of violated agreements: words given, then broken.[16]

Strasbourg
March 30, 1944

I've thought long and hard about the existing possibilities after the total defeat I expect we are facing.

1. England and America will be able to head off the Russian and occupy Germany all the way to the East. In this case the result would be partition into many small states. This would eliminate Germany as a political and economic power for the foreseeable future. For that to happen, the West would have to capitulate while the East would have to be held as long as possible. But I have the feeling that the fight against the guys in tuxedoes[17] is more important to H. than the battle against the Russian scum. The result is that, dizzy-headed as he is, he's weakening the east in order to hold England and America in check for as long as possible. Time will tell whether my feeling is right.

2. The Russian will penetrate deep within Germany while the Englishman and the American are slower to advance so that Bolshevism will spread further to the west. This would mean the end of an elevated class, although not the end of the nation—seen in numbers and not in terms of quality. Together with Austria, we're a people of 80 million, and we've lost maybe six million people on the battlefield and in bombing raids. If four to five million "bourgeois" are eliminated, there'll still be 70 million Germans left. Even in the wake of chaos and bloodbaths, this people would still be a political entity, albeit one under the sway of Moscow. In this case, there cannot be the slightest doubt that, in time, this state would become a power together with the Red Army, which would increase Stalin's might.

We—which is to say my class of people—will not experience any of this, at least insofar as the human imagination can envision, but it's nonsense to assume in the latter case that we would become a people of fellahin, as Spengler predicted.[18] No one would be less likely to welcome this development than England and America, even if a thinking person has to admit that it is possible . . . You could even say that, were this scenario to come to pass, England and America would have waged the war in vain, since only weakening Germany for five or ten years would be historically insignificant.

It is not inconceivable that we could reach agreement with England and America if a revolution on our part pushed aside the regime. We would, however, have to give up all opportunities for exercising power such as our army and centralized economy. Thus, when one extends these thoughts to their logical conclusion, one arrives at the following result.

Anyone for whom power politics is the be-all and end-all, as we learned to think from Bismarck,[19] would prefer the second scenario. The embarrassment of being shot in the head or expiring in a concentration camp notwithstanding, the second scenario would not remove any possibility of our remaining a power.

Moreover, *if* we are bolshevized, then all of Europe will be as well. So hurry up with your invasion before it's too late, you Western democracies, assuming you want to save Europe.

Strasbourg
April 4, 1944

In the east, nothing absolutely decisive has happened, if you don't consider Army Group A's wholesale abandonment of the Ukraine as tipping the decision against us. I'm including a newspaper from April 2 that contains a speech by Dr. Goebbels and an analysis of the third phase of the war from his junior, but no less impertinent colleague [Franz] Moraller.[20] They simply must be preserved. The great demagogue once again draws comparisons with the struggle for power before 1933 and claims that not numbers, but strength of spirit will determine the outcome of the battle. Given that tanks and planes, and not big mouths on the streets and at insane election rallies, are the determining factors, such statements are an outrage. How much more are we poor people going to have to swallow before such speeches and essays are revealed to be ridiculous soap bubbles. By the way, he also promises brilliant things to come soon from the German side. We'll just wait and see—and remember those words if the Russian offensive continues.

Mr. Moraller is equally bold when he says that "everything is still possible." Unfortunately, that's also the case for our enemies. Indeed, I fear that they will be able to achieve the very worst.

Moraller has the audacity to propose that the catastrophic phase came to an end on November 9, 1943. For my part, as a humble ethnic comrade,[21] I would contend that it only truly got underway in 1944. But given our horrific state of the southern part of the eastern front, it will remain M.'s eternal secret how he could describe our strategic position as improving after November 9, 1943.[22]

The only thing you can say in light of these articles, inspired as they are by higher-ups, is that the gods strike blind those whom they want to cast into damnation. At the very least, after they invaded the Czechs, our leaders were afflicted with a blindness that led them to believe they could satisfy other such desires without waging war. On the other hand, given our undeniable advantage of armaments, it seems as though our leaders strove directly for war. And the people don't notice! Although one has to be self-critical. I have to admit I didn't notice it, either, until I was alarmed by Hitler's Saarbrücken speech [on October 9, 1938].[23] People were mentally paralyzed by an infernal propaganda. What's more: why would rational leaders want war when, regardless of how the international community may have been rebuffed, they had achieved the lion's share of their foreign-policy aims? Any reasonable person would have thought that they wouldn't. Amidst Hitler's repeated assurances that he wanted peace, there was no reason to suspect that our leadership would be as demonically possessed as we now have, to our horror, realized.

A row of marching battalions was not able to depart from our reinforcement division for Army Group South, because those "above" couldn't decide where exactly they should be sent. I fear that in half a year, such difficulties will no longer exist. They'll simply be sent to Germany's borders, if not somewhere within Germany proper.

How long will Romania stay by our side? The Russian army has arrived there, and I fear there will be a fall which [Ion] Antonescu will be powerless to prevent. Then Hungary's fate will also be sealed.[24]

The coming weeks will decide. If the Russian breaks through to Iasi and Chisinau and past Odessa, that could spell the end of Romanian resistance.

Then we'll read in the newspapers that all the action is happening far, far away from Germany. We'll hear about a deep flank that we've suddenly formed so that the people won't get the idea that all has been wagered and lost, and that it's now just a matter of fighting to postpone the end.

The people? They silently go about doing their duty, whether as workers or soldiers. If anyone speaks out of turn, it's off with his head. For that reason I can no longer believe—or perhaps I should say hope—for a collapse on the home front.

Six months ago I received a letter from Professor B., who served on the military tribunal in Frankfurt am Main and to whom I had written about my worries concerning North Africa. Unfortunately, I no longer have this letter.[25] In any case, he wrote that Tunis would, as a matter of course, be held. Where Russia was concerned, in case it did not capitulate in 1943, Japan would deliver the killing blow during the course of the year.[26]

An educated person, a beacon of knowledge, wrote that!

There's no need for any further commentary. The letter itself is evidence enough of the stupidity of which a German university professor can be capable when he ventures outside his area of expertise.

The good man has not answered two further letters from me. I hope he doesn't hold me responsible for the reversals of history or begin to construct some conspiracy legend starting with me. If they didn't make you cry, you'd have to laugh.

Our propaganda has of course found an explanation for these setbacks in the East: Italy. There couldn't be any cheaper excuse.

And while I'm speaking of Italy, I'd like to record something to combat our tendency to forget. In Germany, especially when things began to turn against us in Africa, many people began to advance the following thesis: Against Hitler's express wishes, Italy entered the war like a hyena in order to get a piece (Nice, Savoy, Corsica) of mortally wounded France. It would have been in *our* interests for Italy to maintain its armed neutrality. Hitler's speech on Italy's demise and collapse completely repudiated this comforting thesis—insofar as an explanation by Hitler is even capable of objectively depicting a situation. Shamelessly, H. declared that Mussolini's antiwar advisers prevented the latter from *immediately* fulfilling Italy's duty as our ally and joining the war effort on September 9, 1939.

By the way, my analysis of a possible Communist Germany was bizarrely seconded by Dr. Goebbels in an article in the last issue of *Das Reich*.[27] He wrote there that if Germany were defeated, England would be confronted with a "Eurasian" block whose power it would be unable to match. He isn't even afraid that the *people* will think this proposition through to its logical conclusion. Apparently, he considers them too stupid. Or does he believe that *Das Reich* is only read by people who shudder in horror at this sort of thought?

Strasbourg

April 5, 1944

Today Lieutenant B., one of our judges, opined that only a separate peace with Russia, in which we give back everything we've taken, could save us from total defeat. Then we could throw all our might toward the West to prevent an Allied landing over the Atlantic.[28]

But such a scenario would require Russia's cooperation, and thus far they've given no sign they'd be willing to go along! For that to be possible, we'd need a situation analogous to the death of the empress Elizabeth in the Seven Years' War,[29] the difference being that the war against England and America would know no limits and be fought mainly in the air, where our capacities are few and far between. Within a few years, that would mean the end of every German city.

In our staff—alongside the indescribably stupid captain M., who's in charge of our self-defense and spiritual needs— we also have a new captain who is supposed to train us. He's a professor and spent a lot of time in England, thus meeting all the conditions for an embittered enemy of capitalism. After we got to know each other in the aftermath of a couple of barroom brawls, he speaks very openly with me.

I have the feeling he sees everything for what it is and is less than happy about the tasks he's been ordered to perform. He admitted as much to me. But he's one of those Germans for whom the exercise of political power means everything, that is, a typical German nationalist, resistant to any enlightenment on these issues. History will have more than few things to say to such unfortunate people who keep beating the drum of National Socialism!

The most fanatical of these ideological leaders is a First Lieutenant Ellerbeck of the Army High Command. He's a schoolmaster and a complete idiot, but one possessed with the typically vehement German thoroughness. I'm recording his name because I'll be interested, in the event of defeat, whether I'll ever read it again. The most likely scenario I can envision for him is suicide. In his insanity, he believes what he says and I have no doubts as to his personal integrity.

He visited us recently, but I wasn't able to attend his talk. As was to be expected, the upshot was that our "internal constitution" will guarantee us, fate's chosen people, ultimate victory. Blah, blah, blah. This logical flaw, if one is allowed to use such a genteel phrase in an age of tanks and bombers, leads directly to the intolerably sentimental assertion that there's no way a nation like that of the Germans can be extinguished. Leaving aside the fact that even in case of massive defeat, the majority of the people would still be here, albeit in a terrible situation, those who worship violence like the Nazis do have no business appealing to fate or the Almighty when things go wrong. By God! People who are always talking about the "sharp sword" have to let the sword decide.

Some *Pimpfe* [small fry] from the Hitler Youth are marching through the streets, singing the most revolting of all songs, with the lyrics "Today Germany is ours, tomorrow the entire world" changed to "Today Germany hears us, tomorrow the world too."[30] *One* small consolation: you youths will no longer need to fall in this war. And after the war these presumptuous songs will no longer be sung.

You can understand that marches, those of the SA as well,[31] are quite popular right now. They're a way of making people feel somewhat secure when terrible things are afoot in the world.

The situation is similar amidst the everyday affairs of a staff like ours. The military machine, be it among troops or military judges, runs so smoothly that it's very tempting *not* to look beyond it, for instance to the southeast. The horrifying thing is that the machinery may continue to run even after the conflict has been decided. I'm one of the "pessimists" who think that the die was cast when we failed to defeat Russia and they counterattacked. Of course, the final decision, complete defeat, may be a long time coming. Given the monstrous way in which those in power terrorize everyone else, we can rule out a revolutionary collapse in Germany. So defeat would mean, as I analyzed earlier, the total occupation of Germany after endless fighting. It would mean that we are rushing headlong toward the most extreme form of defeat, even though our fate is unavoidable. In a year we'll know more, assuming that the moment of truth has not in fact already come.

Strasbourg

April 11, 1944

Four days of delightful relaxation at home with nice little trips. H. may have taken everything from us, but he had to leave the mountains and the landscape alone, and from them we can imbibe renewed strength and some consolation.

I am going to include in this diary the lead article in *Der Alemanne*. Here Goethe is not only misused but wrongly quoted: "Stay for a moment for you are so beautiful."[32] When good Dr. Goebbels thunders, "Those of lesser worth have risen up against the bearers of culture," you can only smile and ask with the ancient skeptic Pontius Pilate: "What is truth?"

Odessa has fallen.[33] Gen. Dittmar used cautious language today in talking about the battle of Kovel. He didn't say a single word about Crimea. We can likely write off the divisions there: two to three German and seven to eight Romanian ones. After the fall of Melitopol, it might have been possible to evacuate Crimea without any losses. There's no doubt that these divisions were sacrificed for the awful reason of prestige. It was the same story in Stalingrad—only the level of catastrophe was far greater. What's truly horrible is that any discussion of the "problem of prestige," although damned necessary, can cost you your head since it's considered "corrosive to morale."

Next week, the Court of the Wehrmacht Commander's Office in Berlin, which has jurisdiction, will convene in Strasbourg to hear the cases of several officers who uttered frank criticism and forecast our defeat. I fear the worst for them. The bleaker the situation is for the regime, the more draconian its internal defensive mechanisms become. History will prove these unlucky men right, I fear. The entire judicial reasoning concerning "corrosion of morale" is increasingly divorced from the initial legal logic that created this category of crime. Originally, the idea of corrosion was the literal sort such as practiced by the Independent Social Democrats in 1917 and 1918. One wanted to vigorously combat this in order to avoid a so-called stab in the back from within. For that reason the law demands that, to be convicted, the offender has to "publicly" try to lame or corrode the will of the German people to defend themselves.

Now the law no longer requires that an offender make any such public attempt. It is enough for him to anticipate and approve of a remark becoming public. And the law simply assumes such approval, even when the offender denies it, because he made the statement in question. Otherwise he wouldn't have made it! Of course, there's no doing without the famous "surrogate public theory" either. Criticism of the Führer was and is forbidden under the perfidy law, which mandates imprisonment for anyone who makes denigrating, heretical, or basely motivated remarks about leading figures of state in public.[34] Today such criticism is considered corrosion of morale and countless heads have rolled because of it. It is obvious that this spells the end for the judicial system. But it's equally clear that the leadership doesn't care about justice at all. The leaders are obsessed with one thought: to avoid defeat as long as possible, no matter what the cost to the people, in order to save their own skins.

I'm happy that some justice can still be done within our military tribunals. With the worst cases of desertion combined with criminal activity, there's no getting around serious punishments, but the following case will illustrate that normal military tribunals have indeed managed to preserve their judicial autonomy.

I was called to pass judgment on a poor little Polish fellow from the Katowice region who deserted to Switzerland. From there, he pushed on to France where he was apprehended. In investigative custody in Colmar, he was crazy enough to draw a map of how to enter Switzerland for some of his fellow inmates, who were determined mutineers. This came to the light of day.

We sentenced the poor devil, who hardly spoke a word of German, to fifteen years imprisonment. The prosecutors wanted the death penalty. The commander in chief of the Replacement Army, General Friedrich Fromm, struck down the sentence as too lenient.[35]

The next tribunal also sentenced the man to fifteen years. The result: Fromm again struck down the sentence.

Our judges were thereby used up and the case was transferred to the commander's office in Baden-Baden. An active judge presided, and to his credit, it must be said that the sentence was again fifteen years' imprisonment. That verdict was confirmed in the end. A new S. Zweig could have written a novella about it: "The Case of Rifleman Maliglowka."[36] That was the fellow's name—he'd never gotten above that rank.

You could write whole essays about military judges. There are some true hanging judges among them, although they are not necessarily the judges who take part actively in the war. Indeed you can observe that one of every German's biggest dangers is an inferiority complex. With military tribunals, it's obvious even to a complete outsider that the more nonmilitary a judge appears, the more stern he will be as a judge because he doesn't want to fuel suspicions that he's a "poor and lax officer." Men like these are a true plague. There's one of them here with us in Strasbourg—Christian charity prevents me from naming him—and it goes without saying that he is frantic to demonstrate his National Socialist credentials. Since Stalingrad, I no longer greet people with "Heil Hitler."[37] I simply can't get it out of my throat. But when I say "Good morning," this fellow bellows out "Heil Hitler" in tones so loud they make me shudder. Nonetheless, he hasn't reported me and my valiant judicial inspectors, whom I also greet in the same "bourgeois-liberal" fashion, have yet to report me either. There are still a lot of respectable people around, especially in the army.

The radio is just broadcasting a proclamation by Antonescu. He is urging his army and his people to hold out. But proclamations are no match for tanks.

The worst-case scenario, akin to that in Italy, would be that Romania would not only fall but turn against us in order to court Russia's favor. That would be both the end of Army Group South as well the beginning of our collapse on the eastern front.

Strasbourg

April 12, 1944

You could see it coming, but it still shakes you to the core. The evacuation of Kerch in Ukraine, enemy advances, retreat to safer positions, in short the beginning of our end in Crimea.

I just tuned in to *Germany Calling*.[38] What the program offered, fulsome praise for the invulnerability of the Atlantic Wall, was pathetically weak. It seemed to imply that the invasion was indeed imminent. If the Allied landing is a success, we can only hope that our agony won't last too long and devour further millions of soldiers. And despite all the bad news coming from the east, there's no stop to the speeches and articles about the "global Bolshevik threat." It's enough to send you into a rage. Who paved Stalin's route to the west if not Hitler, with the diabolical treaty of August 1939, which back then was considered a diplomatic masterwork?[39] Everything might have turned out relatively harmlessly, if H. had kept his side of the bargain. But to use the treaty to attack Russia was, as we now know, the beginning of our demise.

Strasbourg
April 13, 1944

Today the Strasbourg newspaper[40] published the following brief report about the last, very intense aerial attack.

"Berlin, April 12. Almost all previous phases of this bitter conflict pale in comparison with the present magnitude of the air war. It is obvious that we are experiencing the final efforts of the British and American air forces, which were announced a few days ago in London and which our enemies vainly hope will realize the goal of deciding the war solely from the air."

Diary entry of April 13, 1944

Qui vivra verra![41]

How misleading this brief notice is. Not even the dumbest Englishman believes that the war can be ended with air raids. But we might want to believe it. Poor Germany. You'll be reading and hearing a lot of different things in the final phase of the war, however long that may last.

Things are declining rapidly in Crimea. My assumption that only two German divisions were affected by the catastrophe turned out to be correct. But can we afford today to do without a *single* division that could have been saved by a responsible leadership?

Strasbourg
April 14, 1944

Today I went on an official trip to Karlsruhe to get some books for us from General Prosecutor Frey. We started talking about how executions of members of the French resistance should be carried out. As I learned from colleague B., the Wehrmacht has thus far put before firing squads all the officers that Reich military courts have sentenced to death. Frey declared that beheading was also an option. I objected to that in the strongest possible terms, arguing that such people were no different than [Albert Leo] Schlageter[42] and that we had to grant other people the same virtues we claimed for ourselves, namely national heroism, no matter how futile or insane it might be. His eyes widened, although he didn't pursue the matter. If he agreed with me but didn't dare to say that, it's a sign of how cowed such officials are. I was glad when our conversation was over.

The last few days I've been reading Daniele Varè's delightful book *The Laughing Diplomat*.[43] I've found a lot of

interesting things in it, such as the fact that in 1915 Mussolini and his newly founded movement Popolo d'Italia pas-
sionately pleaded for Italy to declare war against the Central
Powers.[44] He even received 100,000 lire from the French,
which he subsequently, to everyone's amazement, repaid.
Apparently, at the time of the Abyssinian conflict, Mussolini also tried to enlist the French government, offering to
prevent the merging of Germany and Austria with force, if
Paris gave up its intransigent position [toward Abyssinia].
The [Léon] Blum government, as I read in great detail in the
Daily Telegraph, brusquely refused this offer. When you recall that its refusal helped give birth to the "Axis," you get a
"healthy" fright at the thought of these "power politicians."
They're worse than horse thieves.[45] Destiny saw to it that he
received his just desserts, and in the not-too-distant future it
will also repay the other "power politician" Hitler for all his
shamelessly broken treaties and promises. Nonetheless *we,*
the masses of naive people who cheered the reckless idiot's
first "coup," are still going to have to pay our share of the
bill. Varè is veritable treasure trove. One of the topics he
discusses is the partition of Upper Silesia, during which England backed Germany and France supported Poland.[46] [Ar-
thur] Balfour, however, wasn't particularly interested, and
that's why we came out on the short end of the deal. [David]
Lloyd George was said to be enraged, remarking that giving
Poland Upper Silesia was like giving a monkey a watch. I
wonder whether he'd still say that today.

The fact is that the Western powers, particularly France, did a lot to ensure that National Socialism came to power. If they had been willing to compromise with the [Heinrich] Brüning government in the critical period around '31 and '32, Hitler and his movement would have lost a lot of momentum.[47] Now they complain about the pigsty that is Germany, when what they failed to do helped bring it about. And in the end, a misled people will bear the burden.

It's some consolation to remind oneself of the following. If we can succeed in not allowing the Russians to advance too far west, so that we're occupied by England and America, we'll lose our national unity, but the federal states will remain, albeit in a state of powerlessness on the world stage. They'll get democratic governments, insofar as this is possible. Does that mean German culture is endangered? Not at all. We reached our cultural apex at a time when we possessed only modest power. National unification in Bismarck's new Germany and a creation of an organizationally precise machinery of state might have been a civilizing influence, but it did nothing to improve us culturally. The "sense of power," which was too much for us to handle, made us arrogant and insufferable. These Prussian disciples of power lack any skepticism, irony, or capacity for self-criticism. Never has a more humorless subspecies of *Homo sapiens* than those who have led us since 1933 occurred in such concentrated form. Where slogans and nationalist phrases are considered holy, there's no room for skepticism. Anyone who has experienced the stupid heads of our determined political leaders and their followers at their events can tell that respectable, cultured Germany has been buried. But it's only been buried by these one hundred thousand lamebrains. It will and should rediscover itself when these pathetic leaders are gone. It will be interesting to see whether these home-front warriors will die heroically in the end or whether they'll try to slink away. The way they noisily do battle with their mouths and on paper right now, they should, by all rights, to a man die with a bazooka in their arms. But let's wait and see.

Today after eating in the officers' mess, I went home with comrade Sch.-U. In civilian life, he's a judge at a magistrate's court, and he still talks about our inevitable victory. Still he's an upright fellow and hardly a candidate to inform on anyone. When I estimated the probability the war had been spectacularly lost at almost 100 percent, he replied: But Hermann Göring assured us that we would master the situation.[48] This sentence, spoken by an educated German in early 1944, simply must be recorded for posterity. It speaks volumes. I shot back that while that might be true of some situations, we would certainly not master the situation of defeat. My comrade is fond of me because we're both passionate hikers, so he wasn't angry with me. He seemed more like broken man. He's leaving in the next few days. I would like to know when he comes round to my view of things and if he remembers our conversation today when he does. Millions within the sheeplike herd that is Germany are equally gullible. You can do anything to them, as long as you possess the necessary shameless irresponsibility, when making promises.

Strasbourg
April 18, 1944

Spent the weekend in Freiburg, where it was once again delightful. How long will this separation from my family go on? I left them on January 1, 1940, and it looks like I'll still be with the Wehrmacht on January 1, 1945.

Made plans for vacation. But what do plans mean when every day a moratorium on leave can be declared. That's the reality of the war. The war and the disastrous course the conflict has taken have fully extinguished our personal lives. If you're young, as I was in the last war, that doesn't matter so much. But if you're older, two months are like a year! I was 54 when I was drafted. I'm now pushing 60. Heil Hitler!

Strasbourg
April 19, 1944

When I flip through these pages, I'm struck by their bitter, impersonal tone. It's like a stranger wrote them. I still possess remnants of joy, hope, and humor. But these qualities, like everything else that is fine, have been buried by the war. How nice it would be to shoot the breeze, like cheerful Varè. But just as he belongs to a world that has sunk in time, these pages are written in a world that's been buried and at a time when the word "hope" has hardly any meaning at all. If I attempted to brighten up the tone, it wouldn't be an honest diary, one written not for me, but for my wife and my son, since I don't know whether I'll survive the war.

As a member of the legal profession, I've often thought about how these pages would be judged in front of the law. "Corrosion of morale" does not apply since the diary is absolutely secret—not even the most regime-loyal army judge would dispute that. Nonetheless, if it were to be discovered, it would mean death. I'd be dismissed from my post and handed over as a civilian to the Gestapo for reeducation. That's the equivalent of a death sentence.

I am going to have to be extremely cautious, then, that it doesn't fall into the wrong hands. As an officer, I can hardly keep it on me and, as a military judge, it's hardly likely that I'll be subjected to a search. I've found an excellent hiding place in which to keep it.

Unlikely as it may be that I should be cut down, it might take years for some local to find it in the vacated apartment in liberated Alsace. He'd read it with a smile and an occasional "Well, God damn" on his lips.

Tonight Dr. M. visited us. He had a lot of interesting things to tell about the air raids, which he learned through his job. We know we're in the midst of a so-called bomber program, 78 hours a week, 12 hours a day including Saturday.[49] So when will see the fruits of this program? When all our cities and production facilities have been obliterated?

M. doesn't believe that there will be an invasion. He thinks that destroying our capacity for production is enough for victory. But I think there will be an invasion . . .

1. because without one, we'll be able to hold out for quite a while
2. because it's in the Western powers' interest to quickly occupy Germany once we've collapsed in order to prevent Stalin's tanks from advancing to the Rhine.

So who will be proven right?

Strasbourg
April 20, 1944

The Führer's birthday! A short speech by the general while we ate and had two glasses of wine, which we normally wouldn't have gotten. What might the most hated man in the world be thinking today? How things have turned around since 1940 when it looked as though we would become the lords of Europe.

Dr. G.[50] of course also spoke today, and he assured us that the fact that we have A. H. guarantees our ultimate victory. The people would probably prefer 20 new armored divisions and a fleet of warplanes. Is there any other country in which a speaker is given such a free ride? We'll put up with anything, so the old soldier's saying goes, and it's true.

England has imposed a news moratorium on all Allied and neutral countries with the exception of the United States and Russia. One could see this as preliminary to an invasion. That's if the moratorium has not been declared for other reasons, perhaps as a diversion.

No air-raid alarm today, which could mean a lot of things.

Strasbourg
April 21, 1944

There were in fact aerial attacks [yesterday], but they were directed against poor Cologne.

Today it emerged that [Erich] von Manstein has been put out to pasture.[51] As General [Otto-Woldhelm] Förster of the Sixth Army Corps told us, he was the author of the plan that Adolf adopted of breaking through at Sedan toward Abbeville. Many thanks from the House of Austria!

Colonel General [Walter] Model[52] is replacing him. In 1941–42, as the successor to Colonel General [Adolf] Strauss, he succeeded in saving the Ninth Army from the Russians who broke through east of Resbau. Will he be able to perform further miracles? I doubt it. Ultimately, God always sides with the strongest battalions, especially when they're armored ones, and General Model can't change that fact.

Took my leave today from Sch.-U., who assured me that my skepticism is unfounded. He'd pondered the matter and

decided that such skepticism was a mental mistake. Bravo.
The German mind has been so softened that logical consistency is considered an error in reasoning. If I didn't feel like
weeping, I'd laugh. How will this good man react when he
sees that all is lost? He'll rage against the leadership that led
him down the wrong path, but it won't occur to him for a
single moment that such deception requires someone foolish to be misled. He then spoke of showing backbone. How
concepts get jumbled. If I do my duty instead of pathetically
whining as Dr. Goebbels does in his articles, then *that* shows
backbone, and the more I'm convinced we will be defeated,
the higher it should be held in regard. *He* thinks backbone
is behaving like an ostrich, voluntarily opting not to think
things through to the end, but to paralyze thoughts with
boastful phrases like "We'll win because we have to win."

I consider backbone to be doing one's duty with one's
head held high for as long as one can. Unfortunately it's not
possible for us small-time soldiers to do more—for instance,
by removing this unfortunate regime.

I just finished listening to Dr. G.'s article in *Das Reich*
being read out loud in the room next door. He's come round
so far as to admit that we are now fighting for our sheer
national and ethnic survival. The bridges have been burned.
What he doesn't say is whether this was necessary, whether
our existence was ever really threatened by those who are
now our enemies. And there are no words about being the
lords at a crowded table, like those he formerly used when
we were still deep inside Russia.

It's strange. The German people seem to be suffering from a complete loss of memory. Anyone capable of remembering a thing would *have to* wake up and *see* that the demagogues realize our cause is lost and are trying to sprinkle dust in people's eyes. Hitler's speech *before* Stalingrad[53] and the state of the front today should alone be enough to open the eyes of millions of Germans. Inexplicably, though, they remain blind.

Strasbourg

April 26, 1944

Today I heard a lecture about espionage on the radio. It focused on the open-and-shut case of an armaments worker. He was traveling in a full train car and the conversation turned to the major setbacks we were suffering. In order to lift people's spirits, the worker proposed that the enemy would soon have another thing coming, a secret weapon.

A court sentenced him to a long prison term for irresponsible betrayal of country since the enemy could have heard what he said.

It makes you ask: aren't the scribbles of Mr. Schwarz von Berg[54] (rumored to be a Goebbels pseudonym) in *Das Reich* and Goebbels's own promises of retribution an irresponsible betrayal of country? Haven't *they* alarmed the enemy, who is increasing the aerial bombardments tenfold?

We are trapped in an utter lunatic asylum! And this is supposed to end well! Such legal sentences are a perfect barometer for how badly things are going right now. If the state of the war was anything approaching normal, they would be impossible.

Conclusion: Punch anyone, even a general, in the mouth as soon as he starts talking about the weapon of retribution so that he doesn't break the law.

In *Der Alemanne,* there was an article stating for the very *first* time that given the enemy's massive air superiority, it was eminently possible for him to establish bridgeheads for an invasion. No commentary is necessary.

Strasbourg
May 2, 1944

General Dittmar has now started using the word "invasion" and spoke of large-scale operations on our part that can't be allowed to grind to a halt as was the case in Nettuno.[55] He neglected to point out that there was no way we could withstand a war of attrition in the event of a large-scale landing. *We* can't afford further millions of casualties. Our enemies can. And that's why the final judgment on us has been passed. The sentence is death—with no chance of clemency!

Today at mess, an officer said that in a meeting with his commanding generals, H. declared that we should have a bit more patience (as if we didn't!) and that the enemy would be defeated in a fashion unprecedented in human history.

What he didn't reveal apparently is how he plans to pull off this miracle. One can only ask oneself: is this insanity or utter shamelessness? *I'd* like to give him the benefit of the doubt and say it's the former.

Or does he in fact have a miracle weapon up his sleeve? It would be about time to use it. Anyway, no one knows whether H. ever said anything like this or whether it's just something spread by the Propaganda Ministry. The people lap up such news like a morphine addict who's unable to live without the needle.

A lot of air-raid alerts last week, but no bombs on Strasbourg and Freiburg.

Strasbourg
May 6, 1944

The article by Dr. G., which was read out today, claims that the success or failure of the invasion will decide the course of the war. A bold statement and one he only dares to make because he knows that the people will once again forget everything our leadership blathers in their ears. Let us recall these words when the time has come and the enemy has marched into France. But let's not remind Dr. G. That would cost us our heads.

He also alluded to retribution, when he wrote about "surprises" of which no one is yet taking account. I ask myself whether the poor laborer, who was sent to prison for saying the same thing, will be allowed to hear those words when the news is read out at roll call in the morning.

Strasbourg

May 12, 1944

Today I had a long, frank exchange with my superior military court counselor, who is just as disgusted by the system as I am and is even more pessimistic, given current events, when

Werner Otto Müller-Hill in Wehrmacht uniform

it comes to the outcome of the war. He doesn't believe that
we will be able to hold out through Christmas and thinks
that an invasion will put a rapid end to the war. I don't agree
completely, but we promised that we would both think of our
conversation, should we be separated at Christmas. He was
hoping to spend the holidays with his mother. His level of
insight is astonishing for an active military judge.

We then talked in great detail about military court procedures and he agreed that military court officers should be a
friend to and not the enemy of good soldiers who have made
mistakes. This is the way I've always acted. I've waged a lot
of battles with judges over poor young men whom, if possible, I wanted to discipline with punishments rather than
prosecute to the fullest extent of military law. This is a very
good solution, but strangely enough it's only an option in the
army, not in the air force or the navy.

In handing down sentences, I also try to be as lenient
as I can and, to the credit of the many generals to whom
I was accountable, I've almost always been successful. If a
defendant whom I had charged was acquitted and the ac-
quittal was more or less tenable, I let it go and did not try to
get the verdict overturned on appeal for the sake of "being
right." My antithesis is an older colleague from Breslau. He
is the most extreme embodiment of the Prussian know-it-all,
although he's otherwise a cheery fellow. But he turns into
another person entirely once he puts on a military judge's
uniform. When he'd been the one to raise charges, he treated
not-guilty verdicts as personal and professional affronts. He

couldn't rest until such verdicts had been overturned and kept foolishly appealing, even though he rarely had success, and most of the defendants were cleared again by a new court. He was a typically Bismarckian German with a power complex and other complexes a southwesterner like myself simply cannot understand. He lacks the qualities that make people bearable, if not automatically likeable—humor, skepticism, self-irony, and the realization that people are people, with an infinite number of faults, even when they don starched uniforms in service of the state. Once I opined that I envied him. He was surprised and when he asked why, I told him that throughout his life he'd always been right and I'd almost always been wrong. He smiled, flattered, understanding not a word I said.

There's a world of difference between me and fellows like this. He's the ideal representative of the docile, order-obsessed, consistent-to-the-point-of-idiocy National Socialist, for whom any criticism of one's superiors is unthinkable. And while he may be the best, most loving husband and father, he's capable to rendering the most cold-blooded and harshest verdicts possible. This devil reveals the German for what he truly is.

Strasbourg
May 24, 1944

A new offensive has started in Italy. That should put the masses in motion.

Today after dinner and a game of chess, I had an interesting conversation with the SS officer in my division. Knowing that he could trust me, he was very open and admitted that our post-1938 policies were aimed at a war to "cement once and for all" that which we had won without a fight: Austria, Sudetenland, the Czech territories. He kept repeating the outrageous new slogan that this war is our "destiny," since without a victorious war over the [Western] democracies we would not have been able to halt Germany's economic strangulation. I objected that the beginning of the international effort to boycott and choke off Germany was our own policy toward Jews.[56] He admitted that this was the case, but claimed the latter had been unavoidable.

What is one supposed to say to that? It seems that our propaganda, repeated incessantly, has made a fool out of a thinking man and an obsessive out of a well-balanced mind.

These cheap formulas about "destiny" are enough to drive me into a rage. But our lean rations don't allow for such emotional extravagances.

Perhaps the officer agreed fully with me and was only defending a lost outpost out of a sense of duty. The man is highly educated and has an excellent sense of humor, so that I'm more and more inclined to think that he doesn't dare, on general principle, to admit what he recognizes to be true. What will his destiny be like? After our defeat, he'll probably spend most of his days as a professor, if he's not considered a war criminal and treated accordingly. I think a lot about the question of what will happen with the millions of Nazi Party comrades and their ilk.[57] The public apparatus of the state is so entwined with the party that it's impossible to imagine how the state can be repositioned under an occupation if the occupiers exclude everyone who was active in the movement or a member of the party.

In order to prevent chaos, the rail system, the post office, local governments, and the judicial system and national administration will have to be rebuilt as soon as possible. If everyone who's contaminated in some form is excluded, this won't be possible—unless the occupying armies themselves assume responsibility for administration, and even then they would need some of the "contaminated."

After World War I, the situation was different. Everyone simply returned to his office and resumed where he had left off when he was drafted, so that *everything* functioned. When I returned from internment in the Caucasus and Turkey to Hamburg in 1919, there were additional trains with a capacity for some 2,000 men from the large-scale sea transports. In fact, I rode in a train car set aside for Baden to Freiburg.

In this respect, the defeat of 1918[58] will be idyllic compared to the one we can expect if our troops actually carry out the lunatics' plan of fighting until the bitter end.

I think I've already written this before, but this much I would like to prophesy. Even in the Third Reich, orders have their limits, namely when the troops refuse to "go along." If that happens, the leadership can rant and rave as it will, and the unhappy officers and generals can issue as many orders as they want, assuming they don't acknowledge how sense-less further resistance is and try to get the troops to battle on. Orders carry no weight amidst the general panic of sol-diers who no longer *want* to fight.

It's a consoling thought that in the very final stage things may turn out differently than Hitler and [Heinrich] Himmler imagine,[59] and whole stretches of the country may be saved from destruction. God willing, may Baden in southern Ger-many be among them.

Strasbourg
June 5, 1944

Spent Pentecost [holiday] at home and enjoyed Freiburg as an oasis in the delirium of war.

Rome has fallen, and it's more than a symbol.[60] Mussolini has published an appeal to Romans. Everything he does can only be seen as a tragicomic gesture—although with more tragedy than comedy, if one recalls the waves of applause he once harvested in the city, when everything was going well.

It doesn't matter how rapidly the Italian front collapses regardless of how much our propaganda blathers on about "gaining time." It's only worth gaining time if it allows you to prepare decisive counterattacks. It takes a very vivid imagination to see us in that situation. We're like a mighty oak tree being sawed away at, in some places more quickly, in other places less so. The end result, however, is unavoid-able. The tree will fall!

To deny the aptness of this comparison, no matter how credulous or stupid the people might be, you have to make recourse to arguments about our enemies' "domestic and external tensions." The former presupposes revolutions and the latter estrangements among the Allies, should they not decide the war this year. To this end, critical letters to the editors of English newspapers are cited—the German public laps them up. But they only prove the enormous freedom of expression they have over there! A society that can tolerate *that* in the fifth year of war must be doing pretty damn well.

Today, some high-ranking military judges and several officers from the Wehrmacht Command in Berlin ate in our mess. One of them opined that only a person who listened to foreign radio could be unsure of our victory. I have no idea whether he meant his words seriously or not. If he did believe in his thesis, it's a sign of how hollow his head is. I rarely listen to foreign radio because it's too dangerous, but my thinking apparatus is still working normally, without being externally "steered." The root of steered thinking may be stupidity, which uncritically believes and internalizes whatever propaganda puts forth. But—this is a phenomenon that, as I noted previously, Keyserling identified—the root cause may also be that thought is steered by ideas that are not injected by propaganda, but rather reflect wish complexes. If you realize that, then the bottomless failure of people's rational minds is nothing that spectacular, even if it's completely incomprehensible to everyone else. One of our staff's better wits, Major X., assigns generals and ranking officers, in particular, to this human category. I hastened to add that university professors and lawyers run neck and neck with them.

If this were only a matter of ideological disagreements, such thoughts might raise a smile. But we're talking about the demise of an entire people who, blinded and seduced, became entwined in the most miserable tyranny that ever existed in Germany. Nonetheless, culturally speaking, this phenomenon has a long history. The truly infernal thing about Hitler's politics is that the war he conjured up brought Germany together as a land of common destiny and culpability, and this community solidifies all the more with every horrific crime against humanity committed by its minions and accessories. For *who* is going to ask me or the many millions of Germans who maintained a sense of morality and propriety and condemned this contemptible regime how we stood toward Hitler? It will just be: You're a German. You cheered him on when he was successful and you're to blame, too, for everything.

The most interesting, albeit the most painful question will be whether after defeat unconstrained thinking, as I would call it, is possible once more, or whether it has been buried once and for all and will only give way to any another ideology—perhaps Communism.

Will the masses or at least educated people see that H.'s leadership was an example of not only unmoral, but also miserably poor politics, which mobilized the entire world against us and cast us into the abyss? Or will we simply invent some idiotic stab-in-the-back legend,[61] as is our wont as Germans? Or will we simply blame God?

The question is crucial for people's internal disposition and I doubt whether many Germans, particularly Prussians, are capable of such insight. Ever since Bismarck, their thinking has been somehow "constrained" and they simply can't liberate themselves from the notion that others begrudge us our existence and economic development. Moreover, precisely because the war was lost, they will blame factors like the enemy's superiority, without considering where our foes' greater strength comes from. The horrific thing is that this leadership has created in every upright German the worst imaginable moral conflict. The upstanding German despises this regime of tyranny and its mendacious phrase making, but he simply cannot bring himself to *wish* for us to suffer such a defeat—which would hurt the people much more than our leaders and which may possibly only bequeath us a Russian regime not that much better than our current one. Since it is probably impossible to eradicate the regime from within, given the watchfulness of the Gestapo and the SS,[62] one is forced to hope that we will at least be able to avoid total defeat. But these look more and more and more like fantasies. There can be no doubt that our enemies will be victorious in the end.

Strasbourg

June 6, 1944

The invasion has begun. And the newspaper published a speech by Goebbels, included here, in which he promises that, in case of an invasion, the enemy will be taught a lesson![63]

Strasbourg
June 7, 1944

There's not much to be gleaned from the German reports I intend to include here. According to a radio report from the front, our tanks are rolling. What's happening there is breathtaking. Will our tanks be enough to destroy the bridgehead, or bridgeheads, or will the Allies hold and expand them? In the latter scenario, things look very bleak for us since the enemy has countless divisions at his disposal and his air force is utterly dominant.

In Strasbourg people are storming the bakeries since people think the enemy might parachute in here!

Strasbourg
June 13, 1944

A week has passed since the enemy landed and there can be no talk of his being "thrown out" à la Dieppe.[64] The enemy has control over a stretch of coastline 80 to 100 kilometers wide and 20 to 25 kilometers deep.

At mess, Captain Sch.[65] proposed that we should "lure in as many of them as possible." It's impossible to have a rational discussion with blockheads like him.

This evening, General Dittmar spoke and his choice of words was positively oracular. He had the presumption to declare that the invasion could become a tumor that would suck the marrow from the enemy. I fear that the only punctured tumor will be on our side once the enemy has amassed enough tanks to try to break through our lines.

But D. has no alternative. Our leadership is so caught in a noose of false optimism and lies that telling the truth, even *once,* would be tantamount to capitulation.

Strasbourg
June 20, 1944

Retribution has begun. Missiles have been launched against London and the southern coast. Will the enemy troops be pulverized, as our fantasts predicted, so that the invading army cannot be resupplied and will ultimately perish?

Dittmar is speaking tonight. Perhaps he will address the topic of what effect retribution can have as a *decisive* weapon.

Strasbourg
June 22, 1944

He gave his speech and tried to convince us that the invasion had been a huge miscalculation. On the topic of our new weapon, he said it was disrupting organization on the southern coast and was thus indirectly "detrimental" to the invasion.

What a bunch of empty words! The pitiless truth is that we cannot repel the enemy and have to be content with being barely strong enough to prevent him from pushing forward from Normandy.

Things are also going badly in Finland. Vyborg has fallen and all our major defensive lines have been penetrated. They're all sitting under the oak tree, that symbol of German nationality, in the east, the north and now the west as well. It will fall, unless some sort of miracle happens. But that's beyond hope.

Strasbourg
June 23, 1944

I had an amusing trip to Freiburg in this godless age. I took the train, first class, from Appenweier and struck up a conversation with a Swiss lady. Next to me a very well-dressed, middle-aged civilian sat sleeping. A book he had been reading lay between us. I glanced at the title, and lo and behold, it was Goethe's *Wilhelm Meister*.[66] When the man awoke and heard the Swiss lady and me talking, he said he was traveling to Ascona, Switzerland. I was dumbfounded, but he showed me his visa, which looked entirely valid. He had tried for three months to get it, he assured me.

When I alighted from the train in Freiburg, I wished him a pleasant journey. I couldn't help but remark that nowadays a person who was well-dressed and reading *Wilhelm Meister*, and traveling to Ascona to boot, was bound to attract suspicion.[67] He responded with a smile. It's amazing that something like this still exists today.

From the frontlines: The attack on Cherbourg has begun and the Russian has launched an offensive near Vitebsk.

Strasbourg
June 26, 1944

The Russian offensive seems to stretch far to the south of Vitebsk, the same place I marched into in '41![68]

A few days ago, our former divisional judge and superior counselor B. visited us. He's stationed in Minsk near where Army Group Center is camped out. Will they be packing their bags or will they hold their lines? Thus far, the Russians haven't succeeded in breaking through at Orscha, having been comfortably repelled by the 78th Division and two other divisions from Baden.*

There's little reason for hope in the west. Cherbourg seems about ready to fall.

The first imaginative newspaper journalist has already written, without blushing, of [our new] strategy of falling back deep in the west.

---

* On June 22, 1944, the Soviet Army launched the massive "Operation Bagration" against the central German front in the East. This offensive drove the Germans from their remaining positions in Soviet Belarus and Ukraine.

There will be much more than that written, unavoidably, when the English and the Americans and the Russians are at the border of Germany. No doubt our leaders will tell us about the advantages of the new, shorter supply lines. Then, one after another, they'll be forced to hold their dirty little tongues because of our unfortunate, *temporary* occupation by the enemy.

Strasbourg
June 27, 1944

The formulations used by newspaper journalists cause me physical pain. Today one of the miserable scribblers wrote that "Mr. Eisenhower's schedule has been disrupted thanks to our resistance at Cherbourg." Considering the useless martyrdom our soldiers are currently enduring, this fellow should be brought up on trial for writing something so crass.[69]

The headline read: "The defense of Cherbourg proves the invincibility of the German soldier."

The truth is: Cherbourg has fallen. Does the written word still serve any purpose at all in the Third Reich?[70]

Strasbourg
June 28, 1944

A lot to do in court since you don't want to have fallen behind at the end of the month. On the last day of the month,

Diary entries from June 28 and July 4, 1944

the statistics from the court are presented to the superior military court counsel of your district and he checks your work very carefully.

Criminality, by the way, is astonishingly low considering that everyone has been drafted. People with 10 to 20 prior convictions are behaving without fault. In a division of around 30,000 men, we only get around 180 to 200 reports of wrongdoing, and most of them are trivial. Only around 40 to 50 cases are brought before the court.

We have no way of knowing, however, how things will be when the blows we absorb become more drastic, when the enemy is allowed through France, or when the Russian is standing on the border to Germany. It's possible that everything will dissolve, and we won't be able to do a thing about it. But I don't really believe that. Discipline is part of the German's very essence.

[Joachim] von Ribbentrop—Hitler's unhappy adviser insofar as H. takes any advice at all—was in Helsingby, Finland. What was the point of this trip? The Finn needs military divisions and not visits from champagne-bearing politicians.[71]

Strasbourg
July 4, 1944

Minsk has fallen! My fears that Army Group South would have to pack its bags have proven justified.

Anyone familiar with the division of military command areas knows what that means! There seems to have been a major disaster in the center. Otherwise the Russians would not have been able to advance on Minsk so quickly.

How will things go on? If this tempo continues, reminiscent as it is of the best of the German offensives, the Russian will soon be sitting on the border to East Prussia.

What will the northern 18th Army do? Will it be cut off or will it retreat while it is able?*

When I think about the final twilight[72] experienced by the Central Army, I recall something strange.

It was during the beginning of the invasion, the second or third day, I think, when my vehicle was pushed off the road and I landed in a ditch. There was an unimaginable rush to the east on the street. Marching infantrymen, artillery, teams of horses, everything pushing forward, as if drawn on by a gigantic magnet.

Suddenly I was overcome by a thought, a kind of vision. What if there was a comparable rush to the west, with us pursued by the enemy? A shudder ran down my spine and I cursed this thought.

But now it looks as though my vision has come true.

Strasbourg
July 6, 1944

Today I heard in staff that the three Baden-Württemberg divisions, including the 78th Storm Division I've mentioned before, are in tatters. The 78th was only recently at full strength, consisting of 20,000 men with the best of equipment.

The enemy seems to have broken through our lines to the right and left of them so that they were simply surrounded.

---

* Between September 1941 and January 1944 the 18th Army had laid siege to Leningrad. A Soviet attack broke the siege and pushed the 18th Army back early in 1944.

While we were eating in the mess, someone broached the question of whether we could expect a *levée en masse,* should the Russian be on the verge of entering East Prussia.[73] I responded that there would likely be orders to that effect from Berlin, but unfortunately . . .

1. there were no masses left over since everyone able to fight has already been drafted and
2. the masses don't have any weapons.

Everyone agreed that I was right. But it will be interesting to see whether the leadership will trot out this shameful buzzword to try to delay the end somewhat.

Just now I was trying to make a phone call but it took a while to get a connection and so, out of boredom, I counted the number of lines Nazi regional leaders and the party have in Strasbourg. I came up with the following figures:

Head of the civilian administration: 33 offices and
    telephone lines
NSDAP Regional Leadership for Baden: 26 offices and
    lines
District leadership and local groups: 47 offices and
    lines

Sitting in all these offices are experienced warriors who love bullets and yet must repel the enemy from their desks on the home front. So when is someone going to extract them from their foxholes?

Strasbourg

July 11, 1944

Gen. Dittmar has admitted that the center of our ranks in the east has collapsed entirely.

In the division, I heard the following about the measures we're planning. As quickly as we can, we're going to form 15 divisions of which Defense Area VI will be providing one or two. Their motto is going to be: "Up to here but not a step further." They'll be equipped with bazookas and antiartillery grenade launchers. These 228,000 men will be charged with holding back the gigantic Russian army. We can reckon with a very broad front, in which each division will be responsible for around 20 kilometers. And people think that this will work!

At a major conference between Colonel General Fromm (the commander of the Replacement Army), Field Marshal [Wilhelm] Keitel, Himmler, and the deputy commanding generals, Himmler reportedly declared that he would take over the ideological supervision of this division. General Keitel responded that this wouldn't be necessary with the division from Baden since he himself would assume responsibility.[74]

If this turns out to be true, which we cannot simply assume, we can breathe a sigh of relief.

I'm going to include the Sunday essay by Mr. Moraller, in which he writes that the time has not come in the west to destroy or push back the invaders. He should have his head slapped. But nothing is going to change. Shortly before we drown, there'll still be people bellowing about how final victory is inevitable.

Is there a more tragic situation for responsible* people in high places, if such people even exist?[75] It's clear that the political leadership will try to save their heads for as long as possible. But what is it with our leading generals, who can't possibly be so moronic? Unfortunately, it seems that all the active officers know that the end of the war will mean the end of their positions and that there won't be any pensions. Their entire economic existence depends on the war and is only ensured as long as the conflict continues. Can we demand mutiny of them when they know what's coming?

That explains why there be no chance of a violent attempt to overthrow H. and his henchmen. *Before* the invasion, this might have made sense since there was a chance of reaching a negotiated settlement with the Western powers. But now the only possibility is total subjugation and the complete dissolution of the army with the terrible economic consequences that entails. *Now* the war will continue for long as the *common footsoldier* fights.

𝔖𝔱𝔯𝔞𝔰𝔟𝔬𝔲𝔯𝔤

𝔍𝔲𝔩𝔶 16, 1944

I shared my thoughts with Major B., the brightest mind in our staff, and he agreed with me completely. He also shared my view that the fighting will continue as long as ordinary

---

* He wrote, in obvious error, "irresponsible."

soldiers are willing. It's anybody's guess when the limit will be reached. We can't make any reliable prognoses other than that our resistance can't last beyond 1945.

Nothing decisive from the fronts. But it's looking bad, very bad.

The division is working frantically to follow order to form the new divisions. During this time, marching battalions cannot, as has been the practice, be sent to the front to replenish divisions with high casualty rates because they are needed to form the new divisions.

Strasbourg
July 21, 1944

The unbelievable has happened. There's been an attempt, apparently unsuccessful, on H.'s life.[76] The usual propaganda machinery isn't working, as is evident from the article I've included by Moraller, in which he tries to blame the enemy. The fact that this article has appeared *simultaneously* with a newspaper article about a wider conspiracy is truly grotesque. In addition, there are Göring's dishonorable statements. He has no right to talk about generals who have been driven out of the east. The man responsible for all the mistakes, Hitler himself, the man who relieved dozens of generals of their command because they "failed" and who has never been at the front among his soldiers like Napoleon or Frederick the Great, should have been eliminated by his generals. The situation is that simple.

The front page of the Strassburger Neueste Nachrichten *with the news of the attempted assassination of Hitler. The headline reads: "Providence has preserved our Führer."*

A few days ago, I wrote in this diary that a conspiracy like this would hardly be possible. I listed the reasons why not. All the more commendable is the decision, taken to one's own personal and economic detriment, to put an end to this tyrant.

There is no room for ambitious motives given the situation in which we find ourselves. This is a first and probably the last attempt to save Germany. It is truly tragic that it has apparently failed. It's horrible that Himmler has now become the commander of the Replacement Army. He and his henchmen will surely carry out a "purge," compared to which the butchery of 1934 will look innocent.[77]

Strasbourg
July 24, 1944

I heard the following in my division. On the day of the attempted assassination, instructions were issued from Berlin to the local defense commanders, in our case to General [Rudolf] Veiel in Stuttgart, telling them to arrest high-ranking party officials. The addressees had no idea what was going on and were naturally reluctant to take immediate action. The gravest mistake of the putsch was not to involve commanding officers. Those who were involved in the conspiracy apparently did not trust all the generals. So the putsch lacked any real vigor. It seems that Providence does not intend to spare us anything and that we will have to go down the bitter path of total defeat.

The first consequences:

1. As noted, Himmler has become commander of the Replacement Army. Fromm seems to have dropped out of sight completely. No one knows whether he took part in the plot.[78]
2. Since this morning, we are using the Hitler greeting. That will ensure we win the war.

Strasbourg

July 25, 1944

Today Gen. Dittmar delivered a sensationalist speech. He said the conspirators had occupied crucial positions in the Replacement Army and scattered sand in the military machinery so that measures needed to shore up the eastern front were, at the very least, delayed.

It seems as if a stab-in-the-back legend is coalescing—at least for the collapse of the eastern front. Of course it can't go much further than that since our propaganda will tell us, after the miracle of Hitler's salvation, that the invasion has made us *much* stronger and that we'll *now* definitely win the war. But it's enough for a nice little legend, or better still: a lie, since the plan was about removing Hitler and not weakening the frontlines.

When we arrived for duty, a new ordinance was read out about total mobilization in public organizations. No doubt it will stop respectfully short of party organs, given that these fools believe that the inner front is more important than the external one. What will become of you people when our armies are defeated?

Strasbourg
August 2, 1944

I haven't been able to write for a while, but nothing earth-shaking has happened on the fronts. We're in a stranglehold, although on one side retreat is slow, while on the other it's rapid.

Turkey too seems to be distancing itself.[79] The formulation used by the speaker on the radio is unbelievable. The feverish activity of the enemy in the political arena, he claimed, reveals the gravity of their situation as they run out of time. It would be hard to come up with anything more foolish. Our enemies have all the time in the world to put an end to *us*—be it in '44 or '45.

Our propaganda is now bombarding us with the message that we only need to hold out for the next two months until the new weapon is deployed and the tide turned. Every month the people are subjected to new lies and deceptions. Everyone involved in them are criminals who deserve nothing better than death since they have the deaths of hundreds of thousands on their consciences.

As he continually reminds us, Dr. Goebbels sees the fact that the Führer was spared as a decision by heaven that we are to achieve final victory.

I think the following:

Destiny has not allowed H. to abdicate his post in this relatively easy fashion. It has burdened him with the damnable task of being the main bearer of responsibility until the very end.

On September 1, 1939, he perfidiously declared that he would not survive a military defeat. In his megalomania, he never considered how shameless such a statement is. He only spoke about himself, not the 80-million-strong German people he was ensnaring in the war. Now destiny is demanding that he now relieve himself of this responsibility before the last decision has been made.

It occurred to me how little criticism this pathetic speech elicited. When he said back then that we had nothing to lose and everything to gain, it was such a reckless statement that people should have sensed that they were just an instrument in his plans to maximize his own power. Nothing to lose! After our defeat, we'll see what we've lost: millions of our relatives [dead], cities in ruins, our freedom vis-à-vis the rest of the world gone for the foreseeable future. That's nothing, Herr Hitler? You're going to make up for that by firing a bullet into your head?

Finland is also distancing itself, [Risto] Ryti has resigned and been replaced by [Carl Gustaf Emil] Mannerheim.[80]

Strasbourg

August 5, 1944

A list has been published of generals and other officers who took part in the attempted putsch and who have been dismissed from the army so that they can be given over to the mass butcher [Roland] Freisler and the so-called "People's Court."[81]

For the military court system, the name that stands out is General [Paul] von Hasse, the Wehrmacht commander in Berlin and the supreme authority within the "morale corrosion division" of the military courts.[82]

It was a bit of unnecessary propaganda to stress that this was what the army "wished and approved" etc., etc. Of course it was H., lacking any magnanimity, who ordered this repulsive spectacle in order to especially defame the rebels and abandon them to the barbaric methods of the Gestapo and Freisler's bloodthirsty court.

Strasbourg
August 9, 1944

I'm including the report about the session of the People's Court. Later research will be interested in the putsch and historians will need information to compare.

You can already say one thing for sure: one has to tip one's hat to these active officers who put the salvation of the people ahead of concerns for their own existence.

Strasbourg
August 11, 1944

Today, the day when Daisy and Benno [Müller-Hill's wife and son] happened to be in Strasbourg, we came under particularly heavy bombardment. They held out very bravely in the utterly inadequate basement of the house.

Lots of damage in the city center. The small Romanesque tower of the cathedral was hit pretty hard as were the houses on Gutenbergplatz. The beautiful old slaughterhouse has been totally destroyed and the street Spiessgasse is a sea of ruins.

Strasbourg
August 16, 1944

My family has left. After the air raid, their visit wasn't pleasant because we didn't know whether a second attack would follow. Yesterday evening we took a walk through the damaged parts of the city, where we saw, sadly, that the lovely Rohan Palace had also been badly hit.

I have trouble understanding why this had to be. We're talking about the center of a city that definitely won't be in German hands for much longer.

It looks grim on the western front. We can no longer hold back our enemies. Nonetheless, the newspapers blather on about how the decisive battle won't take place until our leadership decides it should.

There's been a new landing on the Riviera. It's likely aimed at delivering troops to march up through the Rhone Valley. Cannes is lost. Earlier we would definitely have fought for the city for weeks. Now it falls with barely a shot being fired.

Here a new staff headed by a general has been established to prepare for the defense of the Vosges. But France will already be overrun by the time the orders have gone through to begin digging for the first fortifications. I fear that the staff will only do its work on paper.

Strasbourg
August 17, 1944

Bordeaux has fallen! How long will we be able to maintain our presence in France? We'll be told, of course, that France is big, that our retreats are insignificant and that everything will be reversed in a few months when the new divisions arrive with the "new weapons." And the empty-headed people will believe such statements without considering:

1. If there are new weapons, they'll have to be available in *raw* masses to *all* divisions in the east and the south since, individually, specially equipped armies won't be able to change the fates of the rest.
2. If experienced, battle-tested divisions are no longer able to stop the enemy, how are hastily assembled new divisions supposed to do this?

Here in our staff we have an active judge who's young and energetic but by no means bloodthirsty. He's a committed National Socialist who was thus far absolutely convinced of our final victory and who steadfastly opposed any thoughts that might have shaken German confidence. He's a fellow who would never act against his own convictions because of orders from above—someone with backbone.

It's terrible to watch how this man, whose five senses are intact, suffers from the ever more undeniable thought that "it could all go wrong" and how he desperately searches for miracles that could avert our impending defeat. He knows what *I* think, but he puts that down to my age and respects my views because he's a gentleman. He'd never turn me in, of that I'm sure. How is he going to end up? Sooner or later, hundreds of thousands of people are going to be suffering as he does, but history is still going to take its pitiless course. As I wrote earlier, it's a bit too late for prayers from the power addicts and disciples of [Alfred] Rosenberg.[83] People like this don't deserve to survive the collapse, and insofar as they're soldiers, they should be killed directly by the enemy, for I fear that they will learn nothing from defeat.

Strasbourg
August 19, 1944

A new order from Himmler: we no longer have Saturday afternoons and Sundays off. This is an example of the most narrow-minded, junior officer's mentality—if that's not an insult to junior officers—and will lead only to tacit resentment. We don't give a "dried-up turd," as we're wont to say, about this order. As has been our standard practice, we have a judge, a notary, and a secretary on emergency duty.

I heard today that the latest round of the draft has increased troop strength by 1.2 million men so that every division will be getting an additional 6,000 men. Many of the new draftees are veteran former soldiers, so that they could be deployed as early as November *if,* and only if, we have enough weapons, especially small arms, for them. But this isn't the real sticking point since bazookas and grenade launchers alone won't make the difference. The large numbers of discharged veterans and people excused from military service shows how utterly we underestimate the enemy's might.[84] If they had been drafted in a year ago, could we have avoided our demise in the east? We might have avoided it *for the time being,* but it would have only followed in the summer of '45. In this respect, as bizarre as it might sound, there was a positive side to our rapid collapse.

Strasbourg
August 25, 1944

Romania has fallen. What I fear might happen has happened, quite quickly, and it means the entire southeast will collapse. Now we'll try to hold off the Russian in Hungary, and soon the battle for "fortress Germany" will begin.

Strasbourg
August 27, 1944

For a while now, I've been living in new quarters and my living space abuts that of my flatmate Major W., his wife, and their children. He's the son of a general and worked as a lawyer in Berlin. We see each other a lot, as you'd expect of people who live under one roof. Today he was just "passing through" my room and I vented my dissatisfaction with our system and our leadership.

After a moment's silence, he blurted out: "My dear man, you're risking your neck saying what you do."

I answered that I was sure he would not report me and that for a person of temperament it was impossible to suppress everything that was stewing within and making me worry. The gist of his response was that it was all for naught and we officers had a duty to accept everything to encourage others in their optimism.

It was difficult to say anything to that. As useless as my outburst might have been, superficial slogans are of equally little "use." The war will be lost regardless of whether I see defeat coming in advance or whether I smother myself in hopes for a final victory. Nonetheless, if every soldier shared my view, the result would be that the war would end sooner than can be expected if millions of soldiers still maintain hopes of victory. In this somewhat heretical sense, you could almost say there is some use in articulating criticism. But it's too dangerous. If you're not absolutely sure of where other people stand, you're better off holding your tongue.

By the way, in this respect, the man's wife is far more intelligent. She clearly recognizes our impending defeat and seems to smile at her husband, who thinks that things will still turn out fine and we'll be trotting out a host of new weapons and the like. Insofar as they're not pigheaded Nazis, the worst sort of creature God ever created, women are much less likely than men to live in fantasies. They live on planet Earth and draw reasonable, if emotional consequences from what they see and experience. It's harder for propaganda to befuddle women than men, which is no great compliment for us.

Strasbourg
August 29, 1944

Today Daisy is departing Strasbourg with my "peace baggage." Since there was no handler available, we brought it to the railway station ourselves with a hand-drawn wagon. It's the first one I've ever pushed and pulled myself—but perhaps not the last. No wonder that it was more the cart pushing and pulling me than vice versa. How times have changed. You used to give your golf bag to a porter who would bring it to your taxi. Today, you push your own baggage to the railway station. In any case, the operation was a success because we set out shortly after 6 A.M. At 7 we had checked the bags, just as the same line started forming behind us that had frightened us off the previous evening. But everything went smoothly. How long will we be able to say that?

She's leaving this evening. I have no idea whether I'll see her again and, if so, when and how, and I felt very sad after we parted.

There's been no decision on what will become of our staff. The only thing that is certain is that we're a training and not a replacement division and that it's our job to supply field units and newly formed divisions. It's entirely possible that we'll be summoned back to the old part of the Reich and will make room for frontline troops. It's obvious to anyone with a brain that Alsace will soon become a battleground and we'd have no business being there since we're not a combat force. That's the situation, objectively speaking, but I have no idea whether we have a division's worth of combat troops to replace us. If we do, we'll be relieved. If we don't, we'll stay here and wait and see whether we'll be thrown into battle. It's questionable whether six military judges would be needed for that. A fighting division normally only has one. Given the fact that we're all aged 59 to 67, it would hardly be opportune to deploy us elsewhere. There are other military judges for that. I can almost imagine them discharging us old boys. As we yield France, a process that's happening faster and faster, more and more field command offices are being dissolved, which means countless judges are being freed up. You need only imagine how many were stationed in Paris.

No matter how rapidly military events in the west are taking place, the war machine on the home front continues to work at its slow and steady "peacetime" pace. It's impossible to imagine but now that we no longer know whether the enemy will be at our border in a matter of weeks, my court has been placed under a new jurisdiction, after five years in the same one. One doesn't know whether to laugh or be dumbfounded at this process, which never seems to look at the outside world.

Things look truly terrible at the front! In the west, I see the situation as follows: Blaskowitz's entire army,[85] which was entrusted with the line from Biarritz to Brittany, is retreating through rebellious southern and central France, while the Southern Army is withdrawing through the Rhone Valley.

Within the Army Group North, the Seventh Army, which has been constantly reinforced with new divisions, is being seriously battered and is retreating beyond the lower Seine. The divisions deployed further to the north are likely still on the coast. The English and Americans have crossed the upper and middle Seine and are pressing to the north to attack our divisions on the coast from behind. To the west and southwest of Paris, American tank forces are rolling east and meeting little resistance. The enemy Southern Army is pushing up north through the Rhone Valley.

Today I heard that we're hastily forming some artillery divisions that need to be ready to be deployed in September. Along with their rockets, they are being issued explosives for blowing up their own cannon, which doesn't exactly inspire confidence.

These two divisions with a few other likewise hastily assembled troops are supposed to repel whole armies of tanks!

And the first reinforcements haven't even arrived yet! In Épinal,[86] we have a division similar to mine and I don't know whether we have any more men around. I doubt it, though.

We have a staff led by a general who has praised the construction of defensive fortifications at the crest of the Vosges. Labor troops from Baden, Alsace, and Hesse are supposedly going to be deployed. But will they even get the chance to start digging?[87]

If the enemy's Southern Army advances up through the Rhone Valley and joins up with the American tank forces operating in the south, which we can expect to happen in weeks, if not days, then we in Alsace and southern Baden will be overrun so quickly our leadership won't believe its eyes and ears.

The propaganda march that took place here yesterday and that was led by the gauleiter like the ones back in the "good old days" won't change the situation one bit. If everything weren't so utterly tragic, you'd have to laugh. But the laughter has stuck in our throats and that's going to continue.

Gen. Dittmar spoke very generally today, having effectively *nothing* to say. He talked about innovations in weaponry that had been mentioned by an "authentic" source. So who is this "authentic" source, the speaker's employer, the Ministry of Propaganda? The way our leaders simply toss balls back and forth shows how far we've fallen in terms of experts keeping the people "informed."

Strasbourg
September 1, 1944

Yesterday I received an announcement that I have not publicly passed on but that should be recorded in this diary.

The new head of the Replacement Army, Himmler, has given the commanding generals a long lecture, whose highlight was the statement that Germany's border with Russia has to be moved 500 kilometers to the east since it encompasses ancient Germanic settlement areas. As I understood it, this would include the fruit garden of Europe, the Ukraine. Himmler didn't specify any of the military details with which this plan is to be realized.

One could have just about accepted this sort of thing, had this lecture been held six months ago. But it's simply barbaric to issue commands like this to experienced career soldiers at the very moment that we're collapsing in the west, in the east, and the southeast. Any further commentary is unnecessary. It's bad enough that the newspapers force feed the people with nonsense like this. But it goes beyond everything we previously experienced for the supreme commander of the Replacement Army to do this in an address to his commanding generals. Apparently none of the generals had the courage to obediently ask Himmler how he thought this could be brought about.

Is this a bluff, or is it lunacy? Is it meant to be serious and convincing? This is a difficult question to answer!

Here in Strasbourg, family members have already started fleeing. People were reported climbing in through the windows of the D-Train to Vienna at 2:40 P.M. Superior Field Judge H., who paid us a visit today from Stuttgart, told much the same story about the express train from Mühlhausen to Karlsruhe. And this is just a humble beginning. What's it going to be like in three to four weeks?

There are no divisions in the Vosges. Hitler Youth are supposed to be deployed to dig trenches on the mountains' crest. Soon, the poor youngsters will be subject to attacks by low-flying enemy aircraft. The Reich Labor Service has apparently yet to be deployed.

The enemy has advanced to Toul just before Nancy. The distance between there and here is laughable. In Épinal, there's a training division that will probably be deployed if attacks come from the area around Toul. Maybe this won't happen. Perhaps the enemy leadership will wait for American tank forces to make it up the Rhone Valley before attacking Alsace. That will take around 14 days at the most. These forces are located a bit south of Lyon right now. Ahead of them they've got the remnants of Army Group Felber, which is based in Avignon. If we think about how exposed this retreating troupe will be to enemy bombers on the main street through the Rhone Valley, it's easy to imagine how battered the soldiers will be when they arrive at the Belfort Gap.

According to the last address by General Dittmar, our leadership hopes that these forces will put up energetic resistance. But that's something you can only tell to laymen, not soldiers who know how terrible retreat is and how it eats away at troops' morale. *Where* are they supposed to make a stand, if they're not going to be supported by top-class, divisions at full fighting strength? Where in the world are such divisions to be found?

I just listened to Dr. Goebbels's address about the basis of our trust in which he flatly declared that there is no way of denying us victory. What cheek! How nice it would be to win a war by swinging a good pen, which he undoubtedly does! But ever since Arminius,[88] neither a good pen nor a big mouth has ever won a war, no matter how much fruit those two attributes yield among us. After traveling through Germany in the sixteenth century, the famous writer Michel de Montaigne identified boastfulness as a basic German trait.[89] He described us as bossy and quarrelsome but honest. He knew us well.

I also just heard the daily Wehrmacht report. Amiens and Verdun have fallen, the later with roughly the same speed as we captured it in 1940. Everything is reversing. The difference is that no one is watching our backs. We've definitely lost. I no longer believe in a miracle either in terms of weapons or in a political sense, as was the case with Frederick the Great.

Sunday evening
September 3, 1944

I was back in Freiburg for what's certain to be the last time in a while. In the coming weeks and months there are likely to be attacks on the train stations in Strasbourg, Appenweier, Offenburg (because of the junction with the Black Forest rail line), and Freiburg (to disrupt the Höllental line) as well as on the main rail route through Mülheim, Neuenburg, and Freiburg-Colmar. That will make it impossible to travel back to Freiburg. A civil servant or someone required to work in the field might be able to arrange transport, but not a member of the Wehrmacht.

I felt quite strange when I took my leave from brave Daisy and Benno. Externally, of course, we avoided pathos, but inside it was definitely a different story! How often have we taken leave from one another without any serious worries? Today it might have been our *final* goodbye. I have no idea whether I'll be transferred with my division somewhere else. It is not a fighting force, but that doesn't matter to a leadership that only wants to buy some time. What's more, I don't know if we will survive the aerial attacks to come.

What sort of a situation has our dastardly leadership thrust upon true patriots—in contrast to slogan-spewing fake heroes and phraseologists! Assuming that there's no reversal in our fortunes thanks to some gigantic force, the true patriot must prefer a sudden, hard collapse to a slow strangulation with countless more dead and wounded and further cities destroyed! To say anything else is just lip service. Whether or not the leadership hangs on for several more months is utterly irrelevant to the victims who would pay the price.

This morning some 14-year-old (!) "small fry" marched through Freiburg. They're being sent to build fortifications in Alsace. This is nothing short of a crime against these children! It is clear, and the local leadership who issued the orders knows it, that these kids will soon be exposed to the harshest sorts of attacks by bombers and low-flying warplanes. And *when* that happens, we'll hear complaints about enemy massacres. No one will raise his voice in this system of terror because no one can risk it.

There are hundreds of air force troops and rear servicemen here and in Baden, but it never occurs to anyone to use able-bodied soldiers for this task. A lady with whom I was riding the tram told me that an officer discovered one such able-bodied troupe near Belfort Gap and beseeched the Führer to send them back to the front immediately.

Monday
September 4, 1944

I heard the following today in my division. Two gigantic columns are trekking up the Rhone Valley. The first is *said* to encompass 100,000 people, 30,000 soldiers and the rest support, secretaries, and the like. The second is supposedly 60,000 in number. *Behind* them is the enemy who is pressing forward. Army Group Blaskowitz is supposed to march with the forces located to the south of Brittany to the Pyrenees to delay them. You don't need much imagination to visualize *how* this retreat is being carried out. It just occurred to me there are also 30,000 to 40,000 "Bose Indians,"[90] and some eastern battalions who are also retreating in columns.

I don't know how much of this reflects the facts. If a lot of it *does,* it will be horrible when the columns approach the Rhine since we have to assume the enemy will destroy the bridges.

Within the division itself, we've bizarrely begun to develop into a fighting and replacement division. [Lieutenant] General [Willy] Seeger is in charge of the troops deployed in the Vosges as battle commander and the rest of the division as a replacement commander. In the long term, of course, this is untenable.

General [Otto] Tscherning—our former commander, who was a flawless cavalier and an ideal supreme judge—is supposedly being put in charge of a so-called collection point. That means he's responsible for stopping the troops streaming in from the west, dividing them up and redeploying them. What a horrible task. Where is one supposed to get weapons for these troops? And how to equip them with all the other things troops need, support staff, vehicles, and food?

This would be the moment for armistice negotiations, so that we're not flooded with disorganized armies who cannot be expected to offer meaningful resistance. I foresee chaos breaking out in the not all-too-distant future.

The wife of Major W., the woman with whom I'm quartered, is setting off early tomorrow without knowing where she'll stay. She's taking everything she can carry, but she will have to leave behind bag after bag, crate upon crate. We sat together in the cellar and talked over the situation:

The gauleiters have forbidden civil servants from taking their wives and children to safety. General Seeger "wishes" that they not do this without issuing explicit orders not to. But any attempt to procure a truck to transport luggage meets with *absolutely* unyielding resistance. So most of the women remain here.

A female friend of Mrs. W., the wife of Superior Government Counsel [Walter] Gaedeke, the adjutant to Gauleiter [Robert] Wagner, wanted to take her to the area around Lahr since she has two sick young children. The gauleiter forbade her to! The plan came to naught. But she did inform Mrs. W. that her husband had told her something big would happen in the next *two* days.

She isn't the only person from whom I've heard this rumor. It is circulating everywhere in the west. Himmler, who was in Strasbourg yesterday, said that Alsace and Lorraine "will be held." The past Thursday and Friday, he claimed, were the critical days, and a counteroffensive was in the offing. There's nothing I can add to that! We're living in an absolute lunatic asylum.

The Führer is also supposed to have been in the west—at least that's the word from Metz where the supreme commander west is, or at least was, located. Here in the city, people are saying that Metz has already fallen. [Günther] v[on] Kluge is reported to have committed suicide,[91] and [Walter] Model, the big man from the east, is said to have been designated his successor.

Word that Finland is out of the war is simply accepted as a matter of course by people here. Panic is threatening!

Just now, the girl from the city has brought the news, no doubt heard on foreign radio, that the Englishman has broken through in Belgium and taken Brussels. If that's true, it's terrible news since it spells the end of any final vague hope for the miracle weapon V-3-V-8.[92] I'd like to take the opportunity to speak a word of prophesy.

When defeat has become so obvious that even the stupidest people can't help but see it, our propaganda will invent a stab-in-the-back legend. That's obvious. Nothing could be better suited than the following formulation: The deployment of the V-2, V-3, etc., was planned for a time in which the invasion was not yet in full swing. Owing to the betrayal of the conspirators, the use of these weapons was delayed, and final victory was snatched away from the hands of our leadership just when it was within reach! Count Stauffenberg and his cohorts are thus responsible for our defeat—and not the Führer, whose genius had put triumph within our grasp.

And the people will believe it!!

Just so that no doubts crop up, given that the people have been assured that we are stronger than ever since the conspiracy has been uncovered, the leaders will claim that by the time they could determine the facts, it was already too late. And the people will believe this!

One's own destiny recedes in importance at a moment like this, when a diligent but, politically speaking, intolerably stupid people is approaching its own physical demise, and starvation—inevitable after a long fight like this—begins to set in. Yet one can't help but be constantly preoccupied with oneself. What sort of situation am I facing? I'm a military judge, not someone intended to be part of a fighting force, but rather one of the six judges attached to our Replacement

Army. For the short span of time in which business can proceed as normal, I will dutifully deal with my files. I'm 59 years old. A hundred kilometers away sit Daisy and 11-year-old Benno. They need me very much. And I can't do a thing for them because my duty keeps me chained here.

Given that a division in the field only has *one* military judge, perhaps they will send the older ones among us back across the Rhine to Germany once this pathetic division is deployed. That would mean a lot. For now, that river—whose bridges very well may be bombed out of existence within a week—is standing between me and home. If I do not fall in the war, perhaps I'll be taken prisoner by the Americans. Imagine that: a nearly 60-year-old judge in a replacement division. It's so grotesque that I'd have to laugh, if I didn't have a wife and child. Things were different in World War I. Back then I was single and orphaned.

As things stand, today I had to tell Daisy to leave behind a note telling me where she's gone if she's forced to flee. As a *last* resort, we could communicate via our Swedish relatives. But that's only if foreign mail is getting through.

How simple and almost *idyllic* our defeat in 1918 seems compared to the one we're facing now. Back then, Germany was undamaged. One simply "went home."—although I first had to be released from British internment in Tbilisi in early May 1919. *Now* we're looking at pointless destruction to our west if we keep fighting—which may not be the case if the Siegfried Line is overrun. *I* think that we'll try to salvage something at the Siegfried Line, but that the troops will then flee, flee for their lives, no matter what sort of orders A. Hitler and Himmler bark at them. Sitting at his desk looking at maps, the Führer no doubt sees the situation differently than what it looks like at the front, when the enemy makes his material superiority felt on the ground and in the air.

Dr. Goebbels has written that he was overcome by apocalyptic visions when he received word of the attempted assassination of Hitler. I must admit that I still see such visions. There is no truth to the idea that the end of the putsch means the danger of defeat is over. The fighting may go on *longer* than it would have, had the putsch been successful. That's the only difference. The end result remains inevitable: complete defeat!

It doesn't take much imagination to picture how our end will unfold. If one sees things clearly and objectively, there are only two possibilities:

1. We'll be swept out of France in a few months— pessimists say: weeks—and will try to defend our border with some newly constituted troops. The Vosges will play a role here. We'll continue fighting, although we'll be forced to retreat there too. The fighting will penetrate ever further inside Germany, and we'll draft and arm the so-called "last" man. City for city, the fighting will continue. The only result will be further ruins to go with those already created by enemy air raids.

a. The scenario presupposes that the troops and the civilian populace follow the leadership's order and *truly* fight. The question is whether the leadership will be able to achieve this, when countless tanks roll up and people realize that they're powerless against them. That's the big question that everyone will have to confront. The power to issue orders ends where panic sets in. If panic is widespread enough, commands are useless. I can imagine our leadership destroying the bridges over the Rhine to force its troops to fight instead of flooding back into Germany. But that doesn't necessarily mean we'll fight down to the very last man. There's still something called capitulation.

2. Widespread panic will break out when the army makes it known that we've been driven out of France and that our western forces are retreating back home rapidly so that they won't be able to make any sort of stand. If this gets communicated to the replacement army, we won't put up any sort of organized resistance, and the enemy will move into Germany in quick advances.

In the first scenario, fighting will continue for a considerable amount of time, even if I now reject my previous prognosis that the conflict could continue for years and believe that this *current* phase can only last for around six months. In the second scenario, it will be like a whirlwind when our troops approach Germany again, which can be expected in around two months.

As unworthy as it may seem to a heroic mindset, the second scenario will restore peace and order to our battered homeland far more quickly than if we're asphyxiated village to village, city to city. Saying something like this out loud could cost you your head! But the fact remains: The heroic ideal, which has persisted from the time of Frederick the Great to National Socialism, has been rendered horribly absurd by a war whose decisive criterion is air and tank superiority! The result for our people will be millions of dead and wounded, devastated cities, and complete deliverance up to an enemy who, this time, will make sure they carve Germany up into many harmless pieces. It will be the end of the power politics started by Frederick, extended by Bismarck with *some* degree of moderation (fear of enemy coalitions, security in the east), and now brought by Ad. Hitler to the sort of end he never envisioned, blinded as he was by domestic success and the mobilization of a large people.

Nonetheless, life will go on. We will have to bear our fate and start over like ants rebuilding a hill someone has stepped on. Confined to small states like Baden, Bavaria, Württemberg, etc., we will be denied any power at all. For a long time, we'll be occupied militarily and subject to the whims of the enemy.

The crucial question at that juncture will be whether the people (1) realize that the political movement that cast us into the abyss was simply atrocious, or (2) try to find scapegoats, for instance the generals, and refuse to divorce themselves from the failed politics of the past. This question is so eminently important because in the event of defeat, the party will do *everything* in its power to encourage the formation of "cells" of resistance, if only cultural resistance, and they could yield would-be martyrs to the cause who will push us completely over the precipice.

Another possible and perhaps even probable scenario is that the people simply moan about our terrible destiny, advancing the notion that "Hitler's policies couldn't succeed" because they were opposed by a malevolent world which refused to grant us our "place in the sun"[93] and could hardly wait to ambush and exterminate us? Given that the first alternative requires reflection and painful realizations and self-criticism and the second perspective is simply too primitive, the people will probably turn to the third explanation. It is the path of least resistance, being what we've been indoctrinated to believe not only since Hitler, but since the founding of the German Reich by Bismarck.

It is strange and unsettling to trace the misery caused in our political culture by the idea that others didn't "grant" us anything. I need say nothing about Hitler's Reich, in which this idea was simply a cruel propaganda trick used to "weld us together," as the phrase went, into a steel-hard unit. But even in the Wilhelmine era, it was the rule to glare beyond our borders with mistrust.[94] Might this be because envy is one of our own biggest flaws and we assume the same must be true for other peoples as well?

In any case, it is certain that if reflective contemplation does prevail, the ground for it is better laid among Catholic areas of the population, in Baden, the Rhineland, probably also Bavaria, and even Austria, which lost its head for a bit and behaved foolishly when it joined the empire, but which was soon healed.[95]

Of course it's also clear that after our defeat endless numbers of people will curse National Socialism and our criminal Führer, and assign blame to the movement and its leader. But I dare not to predict whether they will also reflect that this damnable poison flowed into a willfully accepting body!

Strasbourg

September 5, 1944

I was just visited by a lady from Freiburg who asked me to find out from our general whether the 14-year-olds deployed on the other side of the Vosges have been withdrawn. I'll do my best to see that this crime isn't continued any longer. The situation here is not like it is in East Prussia. The Russians don't have anywhere near the same sort of massive air force the English and Americans have.

Those poor boys, few of whom have reached manhood, were drafted last Friday. They spent their first night in a school with no beds. The second night their train was in Appenweier. Where they went after that, no one knows. It's said they've been deployed at Saint-Dié, although there are American tanks between Toul and Nancy.

What an *agony* the Nazi Party is suffering as it goes through its fianl agonies.

In Freiburg, red posters have been nailed up to announce that, as per the Führer's orders, the Siegfried Line is to be reactivated, and all women under the age of 50 and men under the age of 65 will be deployed to complete it. They're to provide their own supplies. But who has enough food for several days? People are also supposed to bring shovels and pickaxes. But who has tools like these?

The newspapers are calling this "the holy war of the people." Has there ever been a more cynical deception? Such desperate attempts to prolong a lost war by a couple of weeks or months should open the eyes of even the most loyal citizens. Perhaps that's a good thing. There is no more convincing way of showing *everyone* that this regime is untenable. But that's *now* irrelevant to the masters of Germany, knowing as they do that their final hour is at hand.

The English have broken through our lines in the west and have conquered Brussels and Antwerp. That will shortly spell the end for the V-1 and V-2 as well.

Now the "foolish people," as the masses are called in China, are putting their hopes in fast fighter planes that will shoot the British and Americans down from the skies and other "new" weapons, rumors of which our propaganda allows out in regular intervals. Fighter planes! Everyone knows that we have a "fighter-plane program," but *how many* planes would be needed to clear our skies?

Here, too, a stab-in-the-back legend will find an explanation for why they weren't ready when we needed them, around the time of the invasion! The simplest thing would be to blame this as well on Count Stauffenberg and his comrades. General Dittmar will speak about this tonight, if he dares. But what does he have left to say?

8 P.M. He had nothing to say! He recalled the obscure saying that the war had now fallen to the *Triarii*,[96] that is to the Landwehr militia responsible for supplying the front. He spoke of soldiers who were now being "tapped" and who would be able to fight more effectively on shortened frontlines than in broad spaces. But he did not have a *single* word to say about the new weapons, although he always alluded to them in the past.

I've never heard such hopeless phrases. His speech contained none of the silly fanfares to battle-ready newspaper heroes, so at least I could listen to it without bile rising up my throat. But he had to conclude with the threadbare, neither provable nor disprovable cliché that a people prepared to fight to the bitter end cannot be defeated. That might have held some water earlier in history when a *levée en masse* was a practicable strategy. *Today,* in the age of tanks and air forces, it's complete nonsense. But it's the only thing commanders have left to say.

This much is clear. Our leadership has decided to pursue this hopeless war until all of Germany is occupied—if the army and the populace go along. The next few months will show whether this is indeed the case.

Strasbourg
September 7, 1944

Out of the blue, I've been taken to sick bay. On the night of the 5th/6th, I suffered a collapsed blood vessel. I blacked out, fell over backwards, and hit my head as I returned to bed after being woken up by a phone call. Thankfully, I was already at the top of the stairs. When I came to, I was lying in front of the door to my room. This happened at around 1 A.M. The military doctor was informed at 7:30 and I got to see him at 1:30 P.M. after his morning consultation hours. If I'd had something serious, I could have been dead by then, but individuals don't count when we're doing our duty for the Führer.

I received the usual treatment. My blood pressure was measured (110/80), some blood was taken, and some X-rays were made. Tomorrow, I'll likely have an electrocardiogram. Thankfully, I'll be spared a colonoscopy and an evacuation of the stomach—repulsive procedures—as well as the notorious contrast enema. The doctors know that my lower intestines have been weakened by a dysentery infection,[97] so they only want to determine what made me collapse. For me that's a question which is easy to answer! The cause is the war. I began blacking out with the reoccupation of the Ruhr Valley. But the doctor wants more and I won't begrudge him his professional zeal.

The bedside radio is broken, so I couldn't listen to the latest Wehrmacht report. The military news in today's paper is that we've evacuated southern and southwestern France and that we marched through rebellious territory. I thought that France was *for* us and there were only a few terrorists of the bolshevist sort?[98]

Strasbourg
September 8, 1944

They took more blood today—God only knows what for. The orderly muttered something about blood-sugar levels. There were air-raid sirens last night and we all had to flee to the cellar. The same thing happened this morning, but no bombs fell. Our procedures in case of air raids originated in the days when

1. We still had air defenses
2. We were still interested in sparing individuals
3. The siren alerts were rare enough that they didn't significantly disrupt people in their work.

None of these conditions applies any more. If the government is determined to wage holy ethnic war and is willing to sacrifice 14-year-old boys, it's complete nonsense to order whole offices and factories to take shelter in cellars every time the alarm sounds. Before long, we'll be hearing sirens day and night, since we'll be on the frontlines.

It would make more sense to do without alarms and re-ports on the situation in the air, and not send people into the cellars when the flak begins. Surely, *this* government doesn't care if there are a couple hundred thousand civilian and home-front casualties added to the millions of soldiers who have already fallen. But considerations like *this* don't set the agenda. Nowhere can the spirit of the police and bureau-cracy express itself so completely as in an air-raid protection area. The absurd measures will still be enforced when the American or Englishman taxies up here in his aircraft. The best thing would be to force the enemy, too, to obey our regulations.

Our intolerable police state always wants to promote this, prevent that, and find out about something else—all the while permitting crimes like assaults, etc. That was always the case, by the way, whether Germany was ruled by the kaiser or the Social Democrat Friedrich Ebert. What we have now is just an exaggeration—everything related to organiza-tion has hypertrophied.

I didn't get to see the doctor today. I'd like to know sometime soon what they're planning to do with me.

Letters from Daisy just arrived. "Holy war" has just been declared in Freiburg. The poor woman registered her-self to dig barricades and was sent to Norsingen yesterday. The brown boss-men will no doubt be especially proud that, in the phraseology of the Third Reich, "the home front has come together to defend itself with fanatical de-termination, unified and unbending, and in unshakable faith in the Führer." Every day, the Strasbourg newspaper now publishes motivational slogans by the regional party leader. I'm including the last two here. They require no further commentary.

Freiburg
September 13, 1944

Our sick bay was evacuated and, luckily, I've been transferred to the reserve sick bay in Freiburg. Furthermore, I was lucky enough to get a truck—that is to say, to be taken along in one. The drive was calm and pleasant, with no fighter planes along the way. Daisy was completely surprised when I arrived here Monday evening (September 11, 1944). Since my medical files have yet to be delivered, I have been admitted here as a "walk-in" patient and go back and forth between two sick bays, both of which say they don't have the authority to admit me for full treatment. Tomorrow, if the forms are to be believed, I'll definitely be admitted to St. Urban. Until my paperwork shows up, I'll live at home. I have no objections to that.

Enemy aircraft, which attack trains with light bombs, have systematically destroyed our transportation systems. The trains can't run in the direction of either Basel or Höllental. The train station had been closed and soldiers who cannot journey farther on have been quartered there. And this is only a minor, gentle beginning! I fear the enemy will launch massive attacks on the station to completely prevent any form of local transportation. They've done this in France. There, we can only move troops at night.

There is no major fighting to the west. The enemy army is completing its advance. Here, we know what our capacities are. No one has any idea how things stand at the Belfort Gap. Allegedly we are making a stand against the enemy south of Belfort to around Saint-Dié. No one knows either whether *we* are the so-called Army of Blaskowitz. Perhaps we account for parts of it. Being separated from my division, I also don't know whether the retreating column of staff assistants has made its way from up from the south via Belfort to Alsace. In any case, it won't be long before the offensive begins, since, as the enemy troops are fully motorized, their approach should soon be completed.

Whether their attack will be successful, whether it will perhaps break through to Basel, is anyone's guess. It will depend on how large the enemy's forces are and how much air power he can bring to bear. The situation is not quite the same as in Normandy. The frontline there was short. Here it is several hundred kilometers long.

Freiburg
September 15, 1944

No major changes to the west. I'm including today's slogan from the regional leader. How lame it is. If he's trying to give people hope, he'll need to be more dramatic than that. "Many a new weapon!" What's that supposed to mean, after the V-1 proved so insignificant? But that's the way things will continue. It's entirely possible that the English and Americans have massive numbers of troops at the ready, should the units now deployed meet stiff resistance and be decimated. They have *capacity* and that's the main thing for them. They can keep forming and deploying fresh divisions of youthful soldiers, whereas we must deploy hastily trained 17- and 18-year-olds alongside the veteran soldiers who've been cobbled together by coming through our reserve divisions. With mathematical certainty, this inequality in potential strength will spell our defeat, even if fierce resistance does slow the enemy advance into our country. The only result of continued resistance will be the destruction of city upon city, village upon village, the devastation of our farmers' fields, and inevitable starvation.

May God grant that this steamroller pass quickly over Baden, assuming it's not possible to halt it at the Rhine. But that's a laughably improbable scenario, as much as one would like to maintain hope.

Freiburg
September 17, 1944

I'm still at home and am enjoying it with the highest intensity. Everything is calm here, except for the air-raid alarms. No bombs have fallen.

The "as if" situation is eerie. One knows that the end is coming, but one doesn't know when. That depends on when

Alsace is overrun, which could take several weeks or just a few. We threw everything we had left forward at the Belfort Gap and further north. This won't be a cakewalk for the enemy, as the advance from Paris to the border was. What I've written about the distribution of the enemy air force is doubtless correct. The American apparently doesn't like to advance without thoroughly bombarding our positions. As soon as resistance stiffens, he will halt and call in more "preparation," that is, softening up adversaries by the air force. On such a large-scale front, it's less easy for 10,000 aircraft to hone in on relatively small positions, as was the case in Normandy. And the air squadrons have yet to be flown over to France because the enemy totally bombed out the airfields and now has to rebuild them.

At Nancy and Épinal and just on the other side of the Belfort Gap, fighting has commenced. It will decide whether the enemy can advance into Alsace. If Alsace is overrun, the Rhine comes next. It at least is somewhat fortified. It will take some time before this line of defense is completely over-run. Once that happens, the question will be whether we can deploy more troops. If we can do this in sufficient num-bers, the fate of the Rhine-Freiburg area to the north and the south will be sealed since it will be become the battlefield. If we are unable to raise more men, at least we can hope that the enemy tanks will pass through Freiburg quickly. As sad as it may be, that would be the better option for the area as it would escape destruction. It's also conceivable, if not likely, that the enemy will temporarily halt at the Rhine, and that the decisive battles will be fought further to the north. If the enemy advances into Rhineland, Hesse, the Palatinate, and Westphalia, we will have no way of holding southern Baden.

All these questions are crucial to our and especially Freiburg's survival.

The mood here is about what it would be if astronomers had predicted that a star would soon collide with the Earth, wiping out parts of our planet. Everyone knows it's coming, but no one knows whether he inhabits the part that will be less grievously impacted. One result is that people are attacking the supplies they painstakingly saved up because they don't know whether American soldiers will arrive sooner or later. Despite this, it's crucial to keep everything together for the eventuality that people remain here in intact apartments after an occupation. The danger of starvation is massive if fighting disrupts the supply of necessities to the masses. In this regard, most people display a lack of imagination and cling to promises from our leadership that new weapons, etc., will turn the war around. Unfortunately, I don't credit those promises at all. Our frontlines are now under monstrously intense pressure. Yet they are still long enough that, should new weapons be utilized in one position, they would be lacking in others.

Here's the situation. A responsible leadership concerned only with the welfare of the people—after all, the leadership is there for the people, not the people for the leadership— would sacrifice itself to prevent the complete destruction of Germany. The fact that our leadership won't even consider this, that it is sacrificing the people to stay in power a bit longer, is the worst form of moral bankruptcy imaginable. It shows how hollow, mendacious, and cliché-serving our entire system of leadership is.

I have the vague feeling that maintaining the food-rationing system can no longer be justified. But later, they'll be able to say: As long as *we* were in power, the people were properly supplied. *Now* you Germans can see what happens when you get rid of your leadership.

It's no laughing matter for whoever inherits this bank-ruptcy. By comparison the Germany of 1918 was a flourish-ing business! Back then, we still had everything we needed for reconstruction. Our cities were intact, the unity of our empire was guaranteed, and inflation was not inevitable but a miserable attempt to eradicate debts that could not be ended soon enough, especially as large-scale industry and investors were profiting.[99]

I'm not getting any more news from my division. I don't know if it's still in Strasbourg or has been sent over the Rhine, which is likely. Unfortunately, Freiburg is too near to what will presumably be the battlefield for them to be sent here. The Black Forest is more probable.

I can even imagine that lots of military judges will be discharged. Hundreds of them from France and Belgium, with their command-level courts, must now be available af-ter their offices were dissolved. Places will have to be found for them in the replacement divisions on the home front. If I knew that the war would soon be over, I would have no objections because I could devote myself to my family at this crucial time. If I'm released from sick bay, I will have to return to my division and, if I'm not released, the sick bay will be moved to the interior of the country since the combat sick bay will take the place of the reserve sick bay.

Freiburg
September 23, 1944

For the time being, I'm allowed to stay at home. I'm being given walk-in treatment and supplemental food rations. The staff doctor doesn't think I'm suffering from liver damage, as previously diagnosed, and believes it's just a case of poor circulation, with exhaustion contributing to my blackout. Because I suffered a concussion, I have to take it easy. I need lots of bed rest and I'm supposed to eat a lot. You could call this the optimal solution. If the patients are evacuated, which can happen every day now, they won't take me along.

I still have no word from my division. I don't know whether it's still in Strasbourg or has been redeployed. Given the current circumstances, the former is more probable since the American's furious advance has been halted.

An officer who came up the Rhone Valley with his unit said that there had been only *gentle* pressure on the retreating column. The Americans had kept a respectable distance (around 20 kilometers) from the troops at the rear of the column so that the entire evacuation proceeded in calm, orderly fashion.

I've reread my diary entries from my final weeks in Strasbourg and discovered that their hopelessness does not reflect the actual facts. Given what I've heard in the meantime, the reason is as follows:

While the Americans do have strong tank armies, they don't possess the fighting qualities of German soldiers. That seems to confirm something a ranking officer I chanced to meet once told me. In his experience, he said, the American does not enjoy fighting against determined resistance. He wants the enemy to be ground down fully by his air force. Only *then* does he attack. If he again encounters fierce resistance, the air force has to be called in once more, etc. That strategy worked at the narrow front in Normandy. But it doesn't work on the whole western front, which is gigantic.

The fact that the Blaskowitz troops were able to deploy at full strength and in orderly fashion in front of the Belfort Gap is a military and psychological miracle that can *only* be explained by the American's relatively weak attacking spirit. But it is also proof of the eternal qualities of German soldiers. What armies, other than German ones, would have shown this sort of discipline under such depressing circumstances!

We have achieved another miracle. We have succeeded in erecting a defensive front from the Belfort Gap up to Metz and on to Holland, and it will take a lot of effort and *fighting* spirit to break through it.

I think that under these conditions, in order to achieve the sort of dramatic breakthroughs that we feared and hoped would be coming soon a few weeks ago, the English and

Americans will have to deploy many, many divisions, including infantry divisions. Armies of tanks alone, of the sort the Americans possess, won't be enough. The infantry has to march in behind them to take possession of the territory the tanks have breached.

One could therefore envision constant fighting in the southern part of the western front, without any quick breakthrough in Alsace, since we can always send up more troops there. With that, the war would be extended for many, many months. An astounding development considering that reputable officers thought the end might be coming in a matter of weeks.

If one were a foolish opportunist, one might hope that if the Americans fail to advance despite significant sacrifice, the enemy will encounter the problem of demoralized soldiers who don't want to fight! But even that would not mean the end of the war, only its substantial postponement. We can hardly expect people to mutiny in hopes that they'll be discharged and sent home. This would lead to stagnation. We would escape being occupied by the enemy, but it would not end the war. Even in this most propitious case, we would still be too weak to defeat the army, that is, to destroy his invading army.

In terms of fighting morale and operative planning, I have significantly more regard for the English-Canadian armies active in the north. They could break through in places there, if their superiority is dramatic enough.

Freiburg
September 23, 1944

As I learned from a letter written by our head judge, our division is still in Strasbourg. It's impossible to tell from the letter whether its presence there will be extended, but it will probably stay there given the undeniable stabilization of the southwest part of the front.

Nothing new from the fronts themselves. At the moment, the American forces don't seem to be anywhere near sufficient to achieve definitive breakthroughs. The front from Aachen to Belfort is simply too long. They'll have to add countless divisions to commence their "march on Germany."

To the east as well, the only place with major fighting is to the north. Apparently, before proceeding through the General Government of Poland and East Prussia, the Russian wants to drive German troops from Estonia, Latvia, and Lithuania. That's already happening in Estonia. It seems to be just a matter of the remaining provinces. But the fighting will be fierce there and the question is whether the enemy's superiority is great enough to overrun us. We too are making major deployments right now, and it's harder and harder to understand where we're getting the equipment and munitions. If they don't break through our lines, it will come to an endless war of attrition, in which we will certainly run out of steam before the Russians.

Freiburg

September 23, 1944

From now on until the end of the war, we will get to read every day about what our enemies plan to do with us after our defeat. As impartial voices, the authors cite the two pro-Nazi newspapers in Switzerland, *Die Tat* and *Das Vaterland*. It is clear that Jewry, which we have mistreated so badly, is determined to get revenge of the Old Testament sort. If they had their way, as many Germans would be murdered as we killed Jews in cold blood in Poland and Russia. Captain S., who's in command of a train station in Poland, told me that every day a freight train arrived with around 50 cars full of Jews who were gassed and then burned. As per the Führer's orders, these trains had priority over Wehrmacht transports. During our advance into Russia, a so-called special commando was sent to corps staff in Velizh. As one of the leaders told my roommate Lieutenant Colonel Kohlscharfer, their task was to get rid of all the Jews. In a small town behind the frontlines, from which they had just arrived, they had killed 200 Jews. *That* is the truth, which unfortunately is not widely known in Germany. And in light of such horrors, which are unheroic, unmilitary, and absolutely un-German, it would be repulsive, indeed nauseating to start moaning about our fate should we be defeated.

Not much new from the fronts. We destroyed almost all of an air force landing division that the English managed to deploy near Arnheim. The newspapers are reporting on this as though it meant that the danger of an enemy invasion from Holland to northwestern Germany were now over. Of course, the elimination of a division is a triumph, but it's hardly decisive enough that everything is now "stable." It was a *coup de main,* nothing more, nothing less.

As I've already written, the English and Americans will have to send over a great number of divisions before they achieve their great breakthrough. But as soon as runways for large bomber squadrons have been built in France, we'll be so blanketed from the air that it will make the difference.

D. E., a doctor in Aalen who visited me yesterday, told me the following, which I am recording here:

1. Not all too long ago, the Führer supposedly told a highly decorated officer[100] and his bride—the story came from the bride—that the people didn't know how close to victory they were! There's no need to say any more.

2. A manufacturer, a long-time party member, told D. E. he should visit him some time and that he would hear some news that would cheer him up. When he did that, the manufacturer said that infantrymen were being issued small handheld boxes. If you pushed a button, planes would fall down out of the sky and tanks would be suddenly frozen in their tracks.

In my opinion these are symptoms of a grave psychosis from which the populace is suffering at the moment. The

*Werner Otto Müller-Hill with his four-year-old son in 1938. The photo
contains the caption: Benno gets* The Tales of Hans Christian Andersen.

belief in miracles is flourishing as never before. I've heard
it said that a *Swedish* fortune teller has predicted Germany
will win the war in 1946 (!) and will retake Paris in 1945.

I have nothing against miracles. The box cited by the
Swabian manufacturer is, together with the splitting of the
atom, the ideal solution. Poor, poor Germany!

Freiburg
October 1, 1944

A sign of the times. In addition to a pair of yellow half-boots,
Benno (11 years old) has a pair of black ones that just came
back resoled from the cobbler. Daisy explained to him that he

should wear them alternately so that they would last longer. He couldn't do that, he responded. His friends only had one pair of shoes, and he would stand out if he alternated between two different pairs. Further commentary unnecessary.

Dr. M. just phoned and told me about things in Strasbourg, which has been badly battered. Apparently bombs were falling everywhere, not just on the train station. The Imperial Palace (405th Division) remains undamaged except for some shattered windows, but diagonally across from it, the Economic Ministry took a direct hit. Its dressed stones exploded out into Vogesenstrasse, making the street impassable. The academy of music also took a direct hit and there were a number of casualties, including the composer Kaufmann and the conductor Münch and his family.[101] There was a huge crater at Roseneck. Direct hit on the house next to the divisional court. The train station looks a mess. All the hotels are closed. There's no gas and no electricity. People get credit slips so that they can get some soup in restaurants with wood-burning ovens. In times like these we see the danger of houses with all the amenities of civilization. In the end, people envy anyone who has a brick fireplace. More and more, we'll be forced to live amidst the rubble like primitive peoples, just as Spengler prophesied. In my opinion, we're already experiencing the decline of the West, when a drunken, uncivilized Negro can destroy revered sites of culture in seconds simply by stepping on a release mechanism.

We in Freiburg perhaps don't realize what an oasis we live in amidst the surrounding destruction. Will things stay this way? It would be a miracle. But the miracle will be use-less, if we become a battlefield and people follow the Führer's orders to fight house-to-house. Then the city will obviously be obliterated by bombs.

What does the government envision in that event? If one battleground after another is evacuated and razed, worn-out masses of refugees will trudge from west to east and east to west. *Where* in the world are they supposed to stay, and how are they to be fed? Right now, this is a hypothetical question. But in the coming months, that can all change, when the war bursts across our borders. The sheer thought of our "clear-ance" of the Rhine and Ruhr valleys is beyond contempla-tion. I believe when things get that far, the populace will no longer go along with plans of evacuation and devastation so that orders will simply dissipate into thin air. If there is to be *any* salvation from absolute destruction and chaos and starvation, it will be that the populace *stays* put. People will have it tough enough as it is.

Today Minister [Herbert] Backe gave a speech in which he assured us that food supplies are secure.[102] That's true, as long as we keep the enemy outside our borders and don't "de-fend ourselves down to the last man," if he breaks through. But will ordinary Germans realize the logical contradictions between this statement and the government's plans? What do we see written here in a magazine? The district leadership has ordered farmers to help dig trenches and build fortifi-cations. With reference to various *crucial* tasks, they were given to understand that this was more important than their own work. But that would *only* be true, if the fortifications amounted to an insurmountable wall, something impossible to break through. Of course, no one thinks that. A few ridiculous trenches aren't enough to stop modern armies with warplanes of this sort.

As fantastical as it sounds, the basic idea of our leadership seems to be that if every corner of Germany defends itself with determination, our enemies' losses will be so great over time that they'll abandon their offensive. But what about our losses in such an endeavor? Will they not be so great that the enemy will slowly but surely prevail? In *that* case, the plan for national defense will condemn the populace to certain starvation. That's why you so often hear loyal citizens say that the leadership *has* to have a retaliatory weapon at their disposal. Otherwise their behavior would be irresponsible to the people. But I've discussed this conclusion often enough.

When Dr. Goebbels stressed in the last edition of *Das Reich* that our best weapon is the unbending determination of the people, it was a bad sign for the existence of the Swabian manufacturer's little box that downs planes and freezes tanks in their tracks at the mere pressing of a button.

Freiburg
October 4, 1944

The newspaper reported today that a major offensive was in the offing against the Ruhr Valley between Aachen and Holland. A sentence further down stated that Aachen, while still under our control, is apparently fully evacuated and 80 percent destroyed.

The fact that the Americans have not taken Aachen indicates that they refuse to get drawn into house-to-house fighting. They prefer to bomb and torpedo living space to rubble. However, that also means that they cannot take *possession* of a city defended in this way. It will be both interesting and horrifying to follow the further progress of such an offensive, which will proceed at a snail's pace and in which everything is condemned to destruction. If the war continues like this, it may go on for quite some time. Without a ruthless will to battle on the part of the infantry, which the Americans apparently lack, rapid, decisive breakthroughs are impossible. That was different in Normandy and Brittany, where the battles took place in confined spaces. *There* it was sufficient to bomb resistance into submission since not 100, but 10,000 bombs could be dropped on a narrow battlefield.

The offensive far to the north will spare us in the southwest significant hardship, leaving aside the continuing air raids, during which will see whether Freiburg has been earmarked for eradication.

Freiburg

October 10, 1944

Last week nothing essential happened in the west, even though there was major fighting at several hotspots in

Holland, near Aachen and between Metz and Nancy. Aachen is still in our hands. Allegedly the city has been fully evacuated. The only ones left are soldiers. Yesterday, it was reported that the Americans demanded that the city be handed over. The demand was rejected, and the remainder of the city will no doubt be 100 percent destroyed. If this story is to be repeated with *every city,* and insofar as the enemy doesn't make any sudden leaps, the war in the west will go on forever and nothing but rubble will remain. What is the evacuated populace supposed to do when war is conducted like this? Will these millions of people be forced to flee from heavily populated areas into the "interior" of the empire? Where are they supposed to stay, and how are they to be fed? Challenges that weren't easy for a city like Aachen will grow immeasurably if people continue to be evacuated. But you won't read a single word about that amidst all the fanfares concerning our "fanatic resistance."

Fantastical reports are being published about how the enemy intends to destroy *all* of German industry (and not just the Krupp sector). I don't believe in this—at least not to this extent. But the citizen who does believe it can claim that things won't be any worse if we defend ourselves down to the last man.

That is how things are in the west, where the frontlines are more or less stable. By contrast, things have started moving in the east. The Russian has begun a major offensive in the Lithuania region against Tilsit-Memel. He has apparently broken through our lines and can now roll on toward East

Prussia from the northeast. Furthermore, the Russians seem to have broken through successfully over the Tisza River and are marching on Budapest. Whether Hungary will be up to this challenge in the long term is anyone's guess. If Hungary collapses, which we must expect, we can hardly prevent a Russian invasion of Austria. *Where* are we supposed to get the divisions we need from, if the ones in Hungary have their lines broken?

Major H., who was quartered with us in Freiburg, told my wife a few days ago that the turn of the tide was at hand thanks to the *Volksgrenadiere* [People's Grenadiers—low-personnel military divisions created in 1944 that were charged with primarily defensive tasks] equipped with new weapons. Yesterday, the newspaper ran an article, included here, about these new divisions. They're comprised of young and old soldiers—an idea as old as war itself. In terms of weaponry, they've been given the antitank grenade and rocket launchers. These are purely *defensive* weapons.

Today the paper broke the news that 70 percent of males born in the year 1928, that is, 16-year-olds, had volunteered for the war. We are being forced to push *children* to the front, while our enemies, especially those in the west, are deploying soldiers between 20 and 30.

By ruthlessly throwing *everyone* capable of fighting on to the battlefield, our leadership is gaining time, since these forces still have to be defeated—assuming they don't flee. But extra time is all they'll gain, unless they can use their fabled miracle weapon. Our horrible end will come in 1945, if it doesn't in 1944. We can hardly assume that our enemies will give up in *this* situation and the final hope of our leadership is that our enemies' armies will mutiny. In my opinion, it is dangerous and futile to count on that.

Freiburg
October 16, 1944

I'm still in Freiburg and will probably be given a clean bill of health at the end of the month.

Aside from the constant air-raid sirens, everything is calm here, almost peaceful. The city is completely untouched, and only those who have seen heavily destroyed cities know what that means.

Today's newspaper called upon 14-year-olds to help construct defensive fortifications, threatening those who don't with the police. It's so insulting I'm including it here.

The paper also published a speech by Göring to munitions workers. In it, he says: "Fate is confronting us with the hardest test ever faced by a people. But if we pass the test, if we prove ourselves, *we will prove that this global coalition cannot destroy Germany, and Germany's victory will be achieved.*"

Not a word any more about the orchards and grain fields to the east or western expansion and reparations for our destroyed cities. It's now a victory if we're not defeated, if our enemies discontinue battle. Couldn't we have had *this* a bit more cheaply? Without the millions of dead and the destroyed cities? Was our ability to do what we wanted in Germany ever in jeopardy?

Göring speaks not a word about a coming offensive with new weapons that will change everything. The situation is obvious from the fact that Göring's public declaration deviates quite damnably from the bellicose fanfares of the party chieftains.

And the terrible thing is that this situation leaves the future utterly open. There can be no doubt.

What our troops are achieving right now in the west and the east exceeds *everything* they've done previously. Our operative reserves are dwindling as our enemies' armies are growing, and still we are never overrun. *That's* the situation today, and that's the way it will be in the weeks and maybe months to come. But it can't last forever. There's no way of reaching an objective prognosis. But can we hold out on three fronts for an unlimited amount of time, when back in 1918 we only had *one* front at which to hold the enemy at bay? Barring a miracle, the idea defies human reason. It makes no difference whether the end comes in 1944 or in 1945. The only results of further battles will be more destruction in our homeland and more dead and injured.

Freiburg

October 20, 1944

They've issued a call for a *Volkssturm,* the mobilization of popular militias for the final battle. This is the logical extension of the attitudes of our leadership, which has decided to fight to the very last. It would appear that the *Volkssturm* is better suited to partisan warfare—if our heavily armed troops have been broken, the *Volkssturm* will hardly be able to deter the enemy. And every soldier knows what partisan warfare would mean for our homeland. Villages and cities, from which partisans could be potentially supplied, would be *completely* destroyed. (Unlike Russia, we wouldn't be able to supply them from the air.) Every square meter of land occupied by the enemy would be devastated.

There's no need for a thinking mind to even comment on this. When a newspaper editorial writer proclaims that we will keep fighting with our fists and teeth, if our weapons run out, it's the babbling of a lunatic who I hope will immediately himself volunteer for the *Volkssturm* or, better still, be a man and join the Wehrmacht.

Let me reiterate what I've stressed before. It would be appropriate to *demand* every form of sacrifice from the border regions, even their total destruction, *if* the result was that the war would bleed to death and come to an end. That might be an attainable goal, if the enemy didn't have warplanes and tanks. But faced with his immense air forces and gigantic armies of tanks, I don't believe in this scenario. And if Baden is obliterated, and the next German region after that, and the next after that, the result will inevitably be the worst sort of mass starvation.

Our propaganda tells us that this would be also the result of a normal occupation. It's impossible to disprove this hypothesis, since we have no specific previous experience. But *general* experience tells us that the continued existence of the populace is *possible,* whereas our leadership's strategy—should the war not end quickly and our occupation proceed slowly—means with *absolute certainty* that we will be exterminated.

Nothing is ever what it's made out to be. Experience tells us that if our regular troops are overrun, the *Volkssturm* won't help, and a partisan war will be impossible. The "people" don't want to fight and die if their situation is hopeless. They want to live. If millions of brave soldiers surrender and allow themselves to be taken prisoner, you can't expect non-soldiers to behave any differently. Newspaper articles may paint a more heroic picture, but in practice, things would be different if our enemies took ruthless measures to quash a partisan war.

That decision will come on the battlefield, it's that simple, and our practice thus far of "evacuating" our citizens out of battle zones undermines the notion of a partisan war. If there are no more civilians in the battle zone, because they've all been spirited away, it's impossible to wage a partisan war. If that's the aim, the strategy would have to be that everyone must stay and form committed teams that attack enemy lines from behind.

Freiburg

October 22, 1944

A commission from the Army High Command visited the hospital and all walk-in patients, including me, had to report at 10 A.M. Typically, we waited patiently for five hours and were "inspected" at 3 P.M. We hardly made a very proud group, and I don't think there was much of a yield. I don't know what the story was with stationary patients, but I can hardly imagine many were fished out. How many able-bodied men can you expect to find in hospitals? And even if they do nab someone, how battle-fit can people be who've already been wounded three to four times?

The main source for the fighting force is, in my opinion, the back-area formations that now have to be withdrawn from France and the east into the Reich proper. If these people are given a vigorous polish, one will probably be able to make decent soldiers of them. But a polish is needed. Four years of back-area service in France, as you hear from all the reports of frontline officers, has a positively devastating effect on conduct and morale. That has to be gotten rid of.

To enemies and friends, the latter being us, this phenomenon has given the mistaken impression that the army's fighting morale is exhausted. That couldn't be more wrong. Astonishingly, the troops at the front are *still* intact, just as they were in 1918. Otherwise, the enemy would have broken through a long time ago.

Aachen seems to be at an end. Its fall is expected imminently. It will take three to four weeks to conquer the city. To make a crude estimate, one could say that there are 40 to 50 cities that will hold out for a similar amount of time before they are taken. That would seem to rule out an end to the war any time soon. And it seems out leadership is pinning their hopes on a point in time at which the enemy leadership will have trouble controlling their own troops.

The enemy has yet to take Antwerp and Holland. Only when they do that can there be any talk of an advance into northwestern Germany. We should assume that the war will go on longer than many pessimists today think and seemed likely in the turbulent days of September. Back then, it seemed possible that the fronts at our borders could be wound up in a matter of a few months or even weeks. *Now* no one is talking about anything like that.

At the same time, it's doubtful that we'll see meter-by-meter warfare to the east. That is our Achilles' heel at the moment, not the west. When the Russian has marched through Hungary, which may happen in a few weeks, it will be next to impossible for us to halt him.

When you consider the pressure being applied to Germany from the west, the east, and the southeast, the German army's fighting strength seems truly miraculous. For this performance and willingness for sacrifice, Germany—and by that I mean the bruised and bleeding populace, not the Nazis—deserves a more honorable peace.

Freiburg
October 31, 1944

I have been released from my treatment in the hospital and am going to join my division tomorrow. In the interval since I left them, they've been restationed at Oberkirch near Appenweier. That town may be quite near Freiburg, but Freiburg is all the more out of my reach. The ban on leave is still in force and the generosity of the staff officers is a thing of the past. It will be impossible for me to come here on Sundays.

These precious long weeks at home make it all the more difficult to take my leave. No one can tell when I'll get to see Daisy and Benno again. Judging from the state of events in the west, you would have to assume that the situation in Alsace is stable, so that there's no reason to expect decisive changes during the early winter. That would mean that the evacuation of Freiburg has been put off indefinitely and that the division staff will remain in O[berkirch]. But that's all it means. It's still possible that the city will be bombed out, although that's less probably in the current phase.

Things are different in the northwest. There, things probably won't remain stable. The enemy seems to have decided to launch an offensive against the Ruhr Valley in the not-too-distant future.

It's entirely unclear what will happen in the east. In East Prussia, the Soviet offensive before Gumbinnen seems to have ground to a halt. But won't the Russian suddenly march on Cracow and Silesia since we've concentrated so much force in the north? How long will Hungary hold? And what about the threat to southwestern Hungary from Belgrade?

All these questions are completely open. But one thing appears clear. We have no reason to expect Germany to be fully occupied *this* winter unless gigantic amounts of new force are concentrated in the east and the west, and we simply lack the troops sufficient enough to oppose it.

In today's *Alemanne* there was the enclosed article by [Heinrich] Anacker, a "poet of the movement."[103] I met him in the east, when the Sixth Army Corps invited him to recite his poetry. He arrived in a soldier's uniform, sat next to the general, and read out loud, to the general amusement of the staff, some formally quite skillful poems about our advance back then on Russia. Later, in conversation, it turned out he was a born-and-bred Swiss and, a renegade within Swiss democracy, a 150-percent committed National Socialist. In my experience, the Austrian Nazis are also more fervent than any German.

If one were to translate the poem published today into prose, the gist would be that further advances by the enemy would mean the complete extermination of the German people and the utter devastation of German soil. It would be interesting to discuss the consequences of this stance with the wild-eyed poet. His answer would probably be simple. If Germans take this radical attitude toward battle, the enemy will *not* be able to march through Germany, but will be contained within a few border provinces, so that the core of Germany will be saved. How easy true believers have it, be they Catholics or Nazis! They are to be envied. At the same time, one would wish that they *all* fought on the frontlines. Then the front would be impenetrable.

Oberkirch

November 2, 1944

I arrived here yesterday. Early in the morning, Daisy and I drove to Strasbourg to get my few remaining things from the apartment. During a stroll through the city, we saw the heinous destruction of the last attack, in which a bomb fell on the Imperial Palace. The city makes quite a dead impression. A lot of shops are closed because people are fortifying the city. It wasn't hard for me to say goodbye. A staff doctor had moved into my apartment. He was in the Sixth Division back when I was a judge in the Sixth Army Corps. We talked a lot about our mutual memories. According to him, of the 63 officers in his area, only three are still alive. His division met its end in summer 1943 together with the 78th Storm Division.

In Appenweier, I took my leave from Daisy, who traveled in an overcrowded passenger train back to Freiburg, and I arrived at 9:30 P.M. I'm quartered in a room in a simple inn at the train station. It's small, but at least there's heat. My chamber is in the local municipal court, an old building that was constructed in the seventeenth century. The chamber is difficult to heat and gloomy, with the walls covered in dark purple wallpaper. I couldn't help remarking that it would be easier to hand down the death penalty than house arrest or prison terms there.

We still do our own cooking and there's an officers' mess in a side room of the large Hotel zur Linde. The food is good. There's more food available in small towns than in bigger cities like Strasbourg. The whole enterprise reminds me of Treuberg in East Prussia when we were marching on Russia. In comparison with Poitiers, it was Sparta and, compared to conditions later in Russia, it was Capua.[104] It shows you how relative everything is.

Oberkirch

November 19, 1944

I haven't been able to write for a while because there was a lot to do today and a lot of chess was played in the officers' mess so that I repeatedly got home late.

I've gotten fully acclimated to this delightfully scenic little rural town, which projects affluence and strict Catholicism. What an oasis in a Germany that has been so thoroughly disrupted! On Sundays, the farmers dress up in the best traditional garb with red vests. Everywhere you see those typically proud Alpine fellows with their Roman noses and long thin heads. When fighter planes pass overhead, everyone stops on the street to watch. Full air-raid alarms seem virtually unknown. Modest preliminary alarms are good enough. On the surface, it appears completely unfathomable that this blessed plot of land could be ravaged by the fury of war, and yet it is possible, even likely.

We have given our all to raise troops for the defense of the Rhine, but on closer inspection, it only amounts to *a single* division between Basel and Karlsruhe, and that's not much, when the enemy will show up with many times that. But right now he's still back beyond the Vosges, where we have five to six battle divisions.

Two days ago, probably backed by [Charles] de Gaulle supporters, the Americans began an offensive near Montbéliard along the Swiss border. The idea was apparently to bypass Belfort to their left and thrust into the southwestern corner of Alsace at Altkirch. They seem to have been successful. It remains to be seen how far they get. Among the army group leadership, one seems to be reckoning with an airborne invasion on the other side of the Vosges. The talk is of four divisions dedicated to this purpose. I don't believe this since there has been scant progress *beyond* the Vosges, and there are no signs of a breakthrough. Only if one assumes that there has been a breakthrough and it's possible to connect with troops parachuted in from the air, does it make since to attempt an airborne invasion.

There has been repeated conversation about major things *we're* going to do in the near future, beginning with the deployment of new fighters that will break our enemies' air superiority to a huge offensive that will push back the enemy and drive him from France.

As I've always stressed, such rumors spread like intoxicating fragrances. People have been waiting and waiting for a miracle that will turn everything around. In the *short term*, we have our hands completely full with trying to check enemy attacks. And that's the way it will stay until . . . there's a miracle.

But it's also astounding how low criminality is among replacement troops. Cases of desertion or grievous violations of military discipline remain absolute exceptions. What we do get for cases are more or less harmless instances of absence without permission and petty theft, in other words, the sort of misdemeanors you find among even the best troops.

Oberkirch
November 21, 1944

I've just returned from the officers' mess, where General Seeger constantly spoke on the telephone. Here's what I gleaned.

North of Delsberg, the Americans and their tanks have broken through the regiment at the end of the wing, and the vanguard of their armor has already reached Altkirch! Rumors that they have crossed the Rhine at Hüningen are false. They arose because heavy machinery, including bull-dozers, was redeployed and people assumed the Americans were coming! What has been confirmed, however, is serious enough, considering that we don't have many troops down there. When the vanguard realizes this, they'll order an air-borne invasion since those troops are guaranteed to be able to hook up with the tanks to follow.

The crucial thing is whether there are large-scale forces backing up the maneuver. If that's the case, it would be con-ceivable for the enemy to break through into Alsace from the south on *this side* of the Vosges, which would trap our divi-sions on *that* side of the Vosges in a pincer, should the enemy also launch a dramatic frontal assault upon them. But even if this isn't the case, they have no choice but to pull back in order to intervene in the fighting.

I can't wait to see whether tomorrow's Wehrmacht re-port mentions any of this.

If this develops into a major operation, it would contradict everyone who proclaimed the southwestern corner was "uninteresting" to the enemy. The war would also approach damnably near my homeland in Baden—although there is a chance that if the enemy were to achieve his great goal of taking care of Alsace, he might wait for the assault on the Rhine and the Siegfried Line, before pressing forward. *From the air,* we would be directly on the frontline, and we know what that means.

Oberkirch

November 22, 1944

During the night,[105] the situation in the southwest was approximately as follows. Army Group 9 succeeded in closing the access canal on the Swiss border so that enemy troops who had pressed that far are for the time being on their own. My assumption that only *one* tank division broke through proved incorrect. There are now apparently two armored divisions and two other divisions, thus four in total, in southern Alsace and we will have to try to destroy them. They are located as far forward as the Colmar-Breisach line.

The general has taken a small staff with him to Mühlheim to direct the battle. What *we,* the 405th Division, can see of this, is of course relatively little. The main forces being thrown into the fighting are from the army group and most likely form the interior.

The situation in Mühlhausen is tragicomic. Allied tanks, around 14 of them, drove up to the barracks of the 56th Battalion. After two of them were destroyed, they turned around, but not before taking the commander, General Hartmann, prisoner. I keep trying to find out precisely how that happened.

Further to the north, things don't look rosy either. The enemy has pressed on via Saarburg to Zabern and is now located south of that town.

Wagner has called for a *Volkssturm!* An unarmed company decamped from Oberkirch. They demanded 1,600 weapons from my division but we had none to spare.

How these poor *Volkssturm* men are supposed to fight is a mystery to me, and it probably is to Mr. Wagner as well.

The idiocy of the very idea of the *Volkssturm* is clearly apparent in this situation. If you can bring together your last resorts into an *army,* it would be sensible. As it is, this is pathetic dilettantism.

Oberkirch

November 22, 1944, 3 p.m.

Events kept coming in Strasbourg. Our superior staff veterinarian and the chaplain were over there this morning to take care of some duties. At 9 A.M. all was calm, and the gauleiter was spouting the slogan that there was nothing to worry about.

At 9:30 A.M., tanks rolled in and shooting broke out in various places. Our two comrades escaped back across the bridge over the Rhine in a truck full of women and girls.

Around noon we heard gigantic explosions so we assumed the bridges were being demolished. Later we found out that it was the gunpowder depot.

There were more gigantic explosions just now, big enough to shake the house I'm in! Perhaps those are bridges?

In addition to the two men I just named, Superior Staff Judge Boll was also over there. He was supposed to preside over courts-martial for soldiers accused of giving up. Wisely, he sent his wife, who lives in Strasbourg, here last night. He is said to have made it back over the bridge, and someone supposedly saw him at 11 A.M. in Kehl.

There are no telephone connections with Strasbourg. No one knows how things stand over there right now and especially *how many* enemy forces have penetrated the city. The enemy seems to have broken through not just around Zabern but also near Schirmeck and we cannot assume that these are just vanguard tank forces. The American is too methodical and careful for that.

By contrast, as I learned in the division, the enemy in central Alsace has been pushed back past Mühlhausen.

Mrs. Boll told me that a stream of refugees commenced yesterday evening—all of them civilians trying to get to safety. I'm very curious what Boll will have to say.

Generals Volk (military replacement inspection) and Vatteroth (Wehrmacht commander) are still in [Strasbourg].

The latter was staying with his staff in the Imperial Palace and is said to have moved to a bunker to direct our defenses.

What's typical of this case, and what causes panic, is how quickly the tanks come. *Without* them, the fighting gradually rolls up to a city and allows one to take a variety of measures. Tank forays turn everything on its head and there's nothing a *Volkssturm* can do about it. Not even infantrymen willing to sacrifice themselves are any good. Antitank weapons are the only things that help. And we're lacking large numbers of those.

9 P.M. Superior Staff Judge Boll returned and reported the following. He was in the Imperial Palace until 9 A.M., when the shooting started. The commandant and his staff left the building, and Boll went to his apartment, in Strasse der Arbeit, to collect his things. As he went back outside, he got caught up in machine-gun fire and took cover. Then he made his way through Strasbourg to the Kehl Bridge, where he was deployed. The *Volkssturm*, which had been given weapons by the gauleiter shortly before, fired upon the German military, shooting from the houses. In particular, a large number of shots were fired from a large house near the bridge. An 8.8-centimeter round of flak put an end to the shooting.

I heard from Major R. that some 2,500 men are still in Strasbourg, a small, totally fragmented group incapable of fighting, as there are many noncombat troops among the soldiers. Senior Field Doctor Schnitzer from the medical department is also still in the city.

We don't know where this pathetic little group has retreated. General Lieutenant [Erich] Volk from the replacement inspection just arrived here. In a bit of black irony, 1,800 Alsatians were supposed to have been drafted today. They're no doubt laughing at their good fortune. The gauleiter has fled.

News from the leadership (political): Today after dinner, our execrable commanding officer read out a speech by Himmler to his People's Grenadiers Divisions. It was held in summer '44. It took around an hour for the speech to be read aloud. A lot of tired phrases about "the duties of an officer." Then the future outlook: [Himmler] declared—and this was read to *us* on November 22, '44—that while the English and Americans had carried out a landing, it had gotten bogged down and could no longer be repeated once it had finally collapsed.

In addition, he said he wanted to move our border 500 kilometers to the east. The things that we get served here can only be described with the good old Yiddish expression "chutzpah."

This idiot, as he proving himself ever more to be, actually thinks he can fight down to the very last man. He'll be shaking his head, as will Adolf as well.

Oberkirch

December 15, 1944

I haven't been able to write a single line until now.

The trip on November 29 was dreadful. We knew nothing specific. In Emmendingen, I met Werle, a lawyer, who was there during the attack and who told me that he had gone to Friedrichstrasse the following day because he was worried about my family. The street had been pulverized. Our house was a heap of rubble and it had been hard to imagine anyone surviving. Once we had arrived in Freiburg, we drove through streets full of debris to the corner of Friedrichstrasse and continued on to number 13. There was no sign of life. No one answered when we knocked and the windows to the cellar were buried. On the way to the Schlossberg bunker, I had a hunch as we stopped at Fräulein Weiss's house. She was home, and the first words she said to me were: "They're safe." They were with the Kraskes. And that was where we saw one another. Daisy and Benno have a room with a kitchen and a bath at Hauptstrasse 23. They got furniture from the Kraffts and the Holschneiders. They've got a roof over their heads. I immediately got "bomb leave" from command and a new gypsy-like life began. But we had each other, and that was quite a lot. After a few days, I was able to go down to our smoldering cellar—it was like descending into hell—and salvage a few things. Some furniture and large trunks, too big to fit through the windows, had to be left behind. Will we ever see them again? For the meantime we'll leave everything in the cellar and hope to find some of it there at the end of the war.

The thousands of people bombed out of their homes are suffering terribly. Panicked people are making their way in a constant stream toward Höllental. Daisy and Benno have the bare necessities and people helped them. My clothes have been saved for the time being and are being kept there. Will they be plundered later? You can't prepare for catastrophes, no matter how clever you are.

Our present is grim, and our future is utterly grim. And we and millions of people who share our fate have the Führer to thank for that.

Oberkirch
December 16, 1944

Today, there was an extensive discussion about our situation. Present were General Seeger's wife, her daughter, several officers and military judges, and I. Interestingly, the women saw our situation as completely hopeless, whereas the men feel we still have some prospects. A particularly clever superior staff judge named Grieb asserted that we simply had to emerge victorious because otherwise history would lose all its sense. I couldn't help but remark, drily, that the other side probably said exactly the same thing.

We were interrupted by news from the bunker that the Rundstedt Offensive [the Battle of the Bulge, in the Ardennes] had begun. The rough upshot was: "Our hour has come. Large attacking armies have moved upon the Anglo-Americans. Everything humanly possible is being done, etc., etc."

Superior Field Judge Esser immediately sacrificed his final bottle of schnapps, and Grieb smiled at me and, for fear of hurting these good, naive "patriots," I didn't dare say anything about the March Offensive in 1918.[106] The parallels are too striking not to suggest themselves.

How will the offensive go? Will it bleed to death after the certain early triumphs? Where are we going to get fuel for our tanks? And warplanes?

In Esser's eyes, the English and Americans have already been pushed into the ocean and we can now turn our attention fully to the east.

General Seeger joined us later and confirmed the news, saying that in the south nothing of it had been noticed.

My head buzzing with thoughts, I went to sleep.

Oberkirch
December 17, 1944

Everyone's talking about the offensive. It's put a twinkle in the eyes of the incorrigible optimists, but unfortunately I no longer number among them. I fear that this Rundstedt Offensive will be no different than the March Offensive in 1918. After some initial success, it will run aground, unless there's suddenly a deluge of German fighter planes and bombs in the sky.

Tübingen
December 31, 1944

My deployment in Freiburg has come to an end. On the 28th I had to move out. It was terrible to take leave of my family. When will I see them again?

As we can clearly see, the Rundstedt Offensive has ground to a halt and become a battle of attrition. The final judgment has been spoken, even for the optimists. Our end is at hand, whether our agony lasts three months or six.

Here everyone is working furiously to organize a new court. It's horribly cold, and you sit in your coat in your unheated, provisionally furnished chamber.

What a New Year's Eve! My home has been destroyed, my wife and child are far away, and the war is marching toward Baden and Freiburg.

I am reading Galsworthy's *Caravan*.[107] It's pretty much the only book of mine to survive, since I had it in my military baggage. Its humanity is a comfort. Accidentally, I stumbled on a novella about an officer who is thrown for a loop financially by the world war and ends up becoming a chauffeur. But "he kept his form." He remained what he was—a gentleman. That's what one has to do now, as a homeless beggar who will be financially as good as destroyed after our defeat.

Tübingen
January 18, 1945

I had so much work to do that I didn't get a chance to write. Work will proceed as usual until the enemy is before our gates. That's just the way it is.

Things have flared up again in the east after the Russian took his time making preparations.

A little while ago, if you wanted to be optimistic, you could have interpreted the calm as a sign that Stalin had "exhausted" himself and had little more to throw into battle.

But that doesn't seem to be the case. Soon we'll witness the Russian invading East Prussia. But will our western troops and our replacement militias in the east be able to bear the shock from the east without falling into crippling despair? The masses of soldiers are what matters. If they refuse to fight, it won't matter if we sacrifice our entire officer corps all up to the rank of general.

The next few weeks, or maybe months, will tell whether there are limits to the exhausted German soldier's capacity for resistance. His strength was thus far nothing short of a miracle. But has the course of the war not forced it to bear such a weight that it will collapse in the end?

Tübingen
January 27, 1945

The end of the month is at hand. For a military court, that means seeing what can be taken care of before the 31st so that the "statistics" that have to be passed on to the higher-ups look good. The head judge in the division was satisfied this time round. We've done good work, even though the final sunset in the east, about which I wrote last time, is now well underway. Poznan has fallen and the Russians have already reached Schneidemühl. How they managed to cover the distance so quickly from back beyond Warsaw is a mystery to me. If their infantry is already in Schneidemühl, they must have been brought there in motor vehicles. Daily marches of that length in winter would be impossible. In an observation about our military situation, one of the "responsibility bearers," perhaps General Dittmar, writes that the German leadership will have to work "deliberately" given the number of spearheads there are. It seems more than questionable to me whether this is the correct word and whether people are working deliberately in the battle zones. The commentaries offered right now are far worse than all the petty, whining babble foisted on us before. Practically every day we're told that an attempted enemy breakthrough has been foiled here or there, and yet that an unimaginable number of enemy breakthroughs continue— at an unimaginable tempo. I don't think the evacuation of the Warthegau[108] was even possible given the speed with which everything happened. East Prussia looks hopeless. As you can conclude from reports the Russian has broken through in the direction of Elbing and our Eastern Prussia divisions are more or less surrounded. Among those trapped is our genial colleague Superior Staff Judge Kolb, who always thought I saw things too bleakly. He simply refused to let his mind work rationally. As so many people did, he thought his way into a world of illusions and wishes. When the Russian offensive in East Prussia stalled, he wrote that the pessimists were wrong *after all* and that the Russian had been left scratching his head. It never crossed Kolb's mind that the Russian pause served to prepare a massive invasion. That's how people are who live in imaginary worlds!

Recently, when I told Herr Gubitz I was worried that the Russian would prepare and launch a gigantic invasion, he replied, superciliously and pedantically, that *we* would now have time to prepare defensive fortifications. And where are they now? Around 200 to 300 kilometers *behind* Russian lines. They were breached immediately.

When are the newspapers going to start inventing a stab-in-the-back legend? I can hardly wait for it! If our grand finale had happened last autumn, the mutinous clique of generals would no doubt have been at fault. But not even the stupidest German would believe *that,* if they trotted it out as an excuse. Still, something *will* be invented. They can't put everything down to the Führer being ill, not after all the denials. Nonetheless, I have no doubt that Dr. Goebbels will come up with the right solution.

Poor, poor Germany. Everyone from the laborer to the common foot soldier to the general has done his duty. But we are doomed to failure by the stubborn hubris of the leadership, who have overburdened the people and the army with simply impossible tasks. How long will it take for the very last German to realize this? One need not curse our leadership—although that's perfectly understandable—to comprehend that *our leaders* and not the people lost the war. That Hitler's grandiose attempt to subjugate the West and Russia and establish total German dominance over Greater Europe failed because of the gigantic scale of the task. That—since for millennia political leadership has been measured on *success*—*this* political leadership has been unfortunate, to say the least. That the way *we* did things simply doesn't work. That our blind underestimation of our enemies, particularly Russia, is the reason for the collapse of the Reich, which did *not* need to go to war, since no one including Russia would have just gone ahead and attacked Hitler, had there not been such a frightful "dynamic." Capturing Czech territory was as far as we could go without a shot being fired. Everything further than that had to lead to war. It wasn't about Danzig and the Polish Corridor. It was about recalibrating the relations of power in Europe.

This unholy treaty with Russia that divided Poland gave Stalin the chance to expand into the states on his periphery while we were tied up in the west. *That* was the core of our misery. If Russia had started to attack its neighbors Poland, Estonia, Latvia, and Lithuania during peacetime, we could have come to their aid, assured at least of the West's neutrality and perhaps their support in the form of war supplies. *This* should have been our policy and war with the West, a risk we undertook because of a treaty with a thoroughly dubious partner, which had previously been portrayed to the German people as a monster and an archenemy of ours. This policy and our entire leadership lie in ruins, and it's questionable how many people will reflect on the things that happened in the past and how many will simply engage in empty blather about how the "others" waited until the time was right to attack us!

As I've written already: Hitler's plan was grandiose, but it has failed utterly. He will be held responsible, but it's a people of 80 million who will be forced to pay with their very existence.

Tübingen
February 3, 1945

Daisy wrote that she's put her name down to be transported to the Stockach area, and I've applied for special leave to be able to help her. According to the Wehrmacht report, Colmar has been taken. And not that long ago, the staff of the 18th Army was in Guebwiller! Things thus look bad there—but where don't they look bad? Since we've withdrawn all our divisions on the right hand side of the Rhine—the First Corps with two to three divisions in Badenweiler and the First Corps with same in Baden Baden—we're helplessly exposed to a sudden attack should the enemy cross the Rhine.

Given the catastrophic reports, the question is whether Daisy will travel by train or wait for the military transport in mid-February. I can't call or send a telegram. I'll have to travel myself if my leave is approved, without knowing what to expect and without any luggage, just a knapsack so that I can remain mobile. If everything goes well, I can salvage some things from the cellar, but what does that mean these days?

The war is coming to an end, that much is certain. It may last several months if our troops fight without respite, but I don't think it will take longer than around three months.

Recently, *before* the Russian breakthrough, whose speed I did not anticipate, I forecast a long war, lasting deep into 1945. The way things stand now, there can't be any talk of that. It's impossible for us to withstand this sort of murderous pressure on two fronts for very long. It seems certain that there will soon be another enemy assault in the west. Where in the world are the "large attacking armies" that Rundstedt mentioned in his daily order of December 16, 1944? Are they in tatters or badly bruised? Where are they? Ironically, I recently heard tell of big plans for the future. A general here said that one or two armies would break through to Abbeville, while another would advance to the Plateau de Langres (1940!) to gain access to Switzerland and cut off everything on the other side! One or two reserve armies were supposedly being deployed to this end. And *nothing* has been achieved other than perhaps getting the drop on an enemy offensive. Lieutenant General Dittmar will of course deem *this* satisfactory in his public speeches, but when he's sitting in his office, he'll be as dissatisfied as everyone who knew *what was supposed* to be to achieved—namely, the decisive turning of the tide in the west. Never has the comparison with the March Offensive of 1918 seemed more horrifically appropriate.

This is a good time for defendants coming up in front of the wartime court. "Front help" is what they're calling our orders. In all cases excluding political crimes and corruption violations, proceedings are to be suspended if there's any chance of the defendant being found partially innocent.

And since we've already begun commuting prison sentences of between two to three years, practically the only rulings we have to make are on the crassest forms of desertion and deadly attacks on a superior. Otherwise, we might as well go out for a stroll. Miraculous as it may be, serious cases are still the absolute exceptions. With God as my witness, it's not the soldier who's a failure—and in our court, we only encounter the most difficult soldiers. It's not the soldier who has lost the war. It's the hubris of our leadership. What a toll was exacted on us by the winter of '41–'42 and our disastrous offensive of '42! Whole armies, first-rate ones, and not just the Sixth Army before Stalingrad! How long are we going to have to put up with this drivel about our ultimate victory? Apparently as long as there's still a radio and a newspaper left in Germany.

It would be interesting to determine right *now* what percent of the German populace still believes in victory. Some weeks ago, it may have been fairly large, but today, the percentage will have become pretty damn small.

I got a radio today and I had just hooked it up when everybody's darling Fritzsche,[109] the ministerial director of the Propaganda Ministry, whose responsibilities included radio broadcasts, started speaking. I only heard a few words of what he said. They sounded serious. He seems to have lost something of the repulsive, Faustian sense of humor that saw the funny side of the war, back when it was so *distant*. Now he'll be able to join the *Volkssturm* and help defend Berlin, should he not prefer to move west and continue his work as a spiritual motivator. I'd like to see *all* these motivators, without exception, do some genuine fighting.

Poor, poor Germany.

Tübingen
February 6, 1945

In order to grasp the hopelessness of our situation, you just have to look at a map of "Greater Germany." The entire breadbasket, to say nothing of the Upper Silesian industrial region, has already been lost. We don't know how long it will be before the bend the front makes along the Oder River will be straightened, but I fear it *will* be straightened. Then all of Silesia will be lost and Saxony will be the new battleground.

And in this situation, our propaganda has the nerve to declare that our three archenemies will try to divide the people and the government as they did in 1918—*because* they supposedly know we cannot be defeated militarily! My dear gentlemen in Berlin, or perhaps further to the west where there's no fighting, the war *has* been lost, and all that's happening now is our death throes. This can last for weeks or even several months, but the final, fatal end is certain. In today's report on our situation, the spokesman—a certain Dr. Krieg—revealed that the enemy's perfidious greed, of which there has been so much talk, has culminated in their demand for complete capitulation. If *that's* not honest, I don't know what is. The sugarcoating for this bitter pill is the assurance that our people will neither be butchered nor enslaved, that the enemies only want to eradicate our leadership. But the government is smart enough to withhold this from the people, encouraging their belief that wholesale slaughter would follow capitulation. Even if this were the case, have we not done the same with Jews in Germany and the rest of Europe? No denial will suffice to suppress it—we've murdered hundreds of thousands of them. After all, "taking care" of Jews who could not defend themselves amounts to murder.

And now that retribution for these crimes is at hand, our leaders are trying to prolong their numbered days at the cost of countless soldiers and the people itself.

Everything we're served up is so dishonest, shameless, and craven, gilded with the prettiest National Socialist phrases, and who knows whether the majority of the people even realize how badly they're being swindled. Only when the last, stupidest Germans (officers, university professors, and senior civil servants not excluded since they're the most philistine) recognize this and see how shameless and dishonest our whole political system and propaganda were, can we expect the people to recover its internal health. Recovery must come within, from our spirit and our heart, and not as a result of the external pressure of foreign occupation.

We failed on all these scores, and even if the Führer constantly invokes the Almighty who determines everything, it is *his own* fault that we lost the war.

General Dittmar just spoke. It was an elegy for the German Wehrmacht. He started by citing the comparison made by Frederick the Great, used over and over, of the high-wire artist balancing over the abyss. Dittmar was honest enough to use it in reference to Frederick's "greater successor." He then spoke of capitulation saying it would lead to an endless terror while fighting on would yield a terrible end. What a lapse in logic. If we are defeated at the end of further useless battles, what will follow the terrible end is exactly what he portrayed as the result of capitulation: terror without end. The only difference will be that hundreds of thousands of people would sacrifice their lives in vain for a lost cause and that apparatus of state would *totally* fall apart while the fighting rages on!

Dittmar did not say a word about ultimate victory, the possibility of repelling the Russians or that the Oder was now Germany's "river of destiny."

Yet even if his lecture omitted a few key phrases, it was as sober as can be expected from someone speaking in the name of the Ministry of Propaganda. If an officer said roughly the same things in the company of some comrades, he could bet his life that he would be court-martialed for corrosion of defensive morale. The comparison with the high-wire artist alone would be enough to seal his fate.

Tübingen
February 7, 1945

A few days ago, I applied for special leave to rescue a few things from my cellar. I was hoping it would be approved because I fulfilled all the criteria, but today I was informed that there is a moratorium on all leave except for deaths in the family. There's no more bomb leave, special leave, or leave before being sent to the front, which was so crucial to troop morale. These are all signs of a regime in its death throes. There's nothing more to say.

Today one of our secretaries returned. She tried to go to Breslau [Wroclaw] and only got as far as Liegnitz. She reported—as I had already imagined—terrible scenes of refugee misery: children and old people dying of exposure during long marches, their corpses simply left lying on the sides of roads. Infants in diapers who literally froze to death in unheated train cars and whose corpses were put in the luggage nets or thrown out the window.

That's not a criticism of the National Socialist Welfare.[110] With catastrophes of this magnitude, organization simply breaks down. The leadership who continued the war when it should never have been prolonged is responsible. They lulled the people into believing that miraculous new weapons were going to turn things around and that German territory would never be conquered. And now there are masses of refugees rolling toward Saxony. In Saxony, there is calm amidst the fighting and yet soon conditions there will be intolerable as well. And what's going to happen when the Russian military machine, which we will *never* be able to stop, presses further on? Are the millions of people now in Saxony going to flee further west? Will the leadership soldier on even then? Although they know that starvation of apocalyptic proportions will be the result? I'd like to pose *this* question to our leadership! But the answer would of course be that there won't be any further Russian advantages. And that anyone who posed such a question would sacrifice his head as a defeatist.

Tübingen
February 9, 1945

When I returned from my duties this evening, the person with whom I'm quartered said that antitank trenches were being dug before Tübingen and that evacuation was being considered if enemy troops approached. It may be madness, but there's a method to it! If the enemy advances this far, the party's power will be over, retreating troops will inundate the region, and all order will be dissolved. Seriously: where are the unfortunate ones who are to be separated from their hometown supposed to go? Where? Don't our leaders realize that the evacuation of the eastern territories has created enough insoluble problems already?

The terrible thing is that every fanatic party leader now thinks he has to prove that he is enforcing the call to defend Germany down to last square meter. If commensurate preparations are not made, one risks being seen as a defeatist by one's superiors. In this way, panic and fear beget insane decisions. No one can take a step back without risking his head. And who is paying the terrible cost? The German people!

At the front, the 19th Army in Alsace has been driven back over the Rhine near Neuenburg! The Wehrmacht report is sickening. It says that, without all-too-great losses of men and matériel, our divisions have succeeded in establishing a narrow bridgehead to the west of Neuenburg. What does this mean in plain language? That the troops have been pushed over Neuenburg Bridge and via ferry back to the other side of the Rhine and that the enemy has pressed forward to the river. Since the good SS divisions formerly stationed on the west bank of the Rhine (the staff of the 18th SS Corps in Badenweiler, that is, across from the Neuenburg bridgehead) are now all posted there, there are no more troops to relieve the exhausted 19th Army divisions.

Further to the north, near Neubreisach, we haven't been pushed back as far, but I fear we'll be forced to retreat beyond the Rhine. And then the question arises: Will the enemy try to force their way over the Rhine or will they be content with having liberated Alsace? One might assume that it would be foolish to march through the Rhineland plains on the Black Forest, which still offers good opportunities for defense and is structured with a significant amount of depth. But how do we know what the enemy is planning?

This evening, an article by Dr. Goebbels was read out. In it, he movingly laments the fate of eastern Germans. Indeed, my good Herr Goebbels. In August 1939 we concluded a treaty to divide Poland with these beasts, as National Socialism always dubbed the Bolsheviks, and it was on the basis of that treaty that we thought we could afford war! Was that an example of good or bad politics? If these goddamn hypocrites and Byzantines would just admit, for once in their lives, that Hitler is only a human being who's sometimes wrong and whose policies back then were—to put it mildly—less than credible, then we could say: political mistakes happen, and you just have to see how you can escape from the resulting mess. But they never do any such thing! Hitler is God. He's infallible, and his policies are the very definition of genius such as neither Frederick the Great nor Bismarck ever embodied so perfectly. Hitler is the man who completes what his predecessors could only begin but not see through to fruition.

That is what's truly horrible, monstrous, and intolerable about our system! They don't even sense that they're in the wrong. If one admits one *single* doubt about Hitler, one will start examining the entire leadership, including the military leadership, critically. And ultimately that would spell the end of people's trust.

Tübingen
February 13, 1945

You would think that the editors of newspapers and magazines wouldn't have an easy time of it these days and that you would notice that fact in their articles and their standard phrases about the war. But not on your life! Yesterday, one of them wrote that we only needed to hold on and things will turn our way because our enemies will see that the German people are undefeatable. Today, another one, or maybe the same idiot, writes that our *tactics* (how dare he bring up tactics) right now are to keep the enemy at arm's length and weaken him ahead of the "decisive confrontation." Where does this pathetic idiot think the decisive confrontation with the Russian is going to come? How far should we draw him into our own country before we decide to destroy him or drive him back out? The third, eternally recurring buzzword is our invincibility, which our enemies are increasingly beginning to see! Unfortunately, those same enemies are well on their way to demonstrating our extreme vulnerability with their weapons! What better indication of this is there than the fact that the Russian is on the doorstep of Saxony and Frankfurt an der Oder?

It's as I always said. Since 1942, we've won the battle of the editorials and our enemies the battle of the battlefields. Nonetheless, editorials will continue to be written as long as there's a newspaper published in Germany. It would be interesting, in an archival sense, to own a copy of the last newspaper with the last editorial. If everything weren't so tragic, you could laugh at the "Hitler Circus." But the laughter has died on our lips for quite some time and will do so even more in the future[111]—and it's no consolation that this will be truer for the leaders of the Third Reich than for us. It may be a question of justice since they alone bear the sort of responsibility that accompanies wielding total power. But the fact that they will perhaps be worse off than the anonymous everyday German, when the war is lost, is simply no consolation.

It would be interesting to know whether they are all seized with fear, true fear. Actually, old warriors and National Socialists aren't allowed to be afraid. Nonetheless, in the past twelve years of total power, they haven't lived badly at all, and that sort of comfort creates *bonds* with this earth. They had their houses, if not estates. It wasn't a sacrifice at all for them to play the role of "cratoplutes."[112] And now that comfort is purportedly over and, with it, perhaps their lives? Actually, all these gentlemen should commit suicide the moment the war is done and the Third Reich is at an end, for they would be unable to breathe in a world other than that of the Third Reich.

If some dumb oaf doesn't bash in my skull because he thinks I'm partially responsible and if I survive the initial chaotic phase that's likely to commence, I will see the answers to the questions I've posed and discover whether our leadership is prepared to die with their heads held high![113]

Tübingen
February 18, 1945

More than ever, the newspapers make me want to vomit! Hardly has the Russian offensive slowed somewhat than they poke their heads back up in revolting fashion! The local rag here had the temerity to conclude an article with the headline "The decision in the east is still fully open"—a concentrate of long-winded, meandering, foolish tedium that could have stemmed from General Dittmar's pen—with the following assertion: "We feel that the Bolshevik offensive can be overcome, if we devote our entire strength to the task. Neither the people nor the Wehrmacht has been annihilated. With that the decision is still fully open."

Dr. Goebbels's article in *Das Reich,* which I heard on the radio today, runs in the same vein. He doesn't shy away from logical somersaults of the worst sort, for instance, when he says that the enemy did not capitulate when we had advanced out into the Atlantic and deep within Russia! No, my good Dr. Goebbels, they didn't. But *they* had a reasonable chance to drive us out, which they have also now unfortunately succeeded in doing. But do we have the realistic prospect of repelling *them?* One only need remember the stalled Rundstedt Offensive to recognize that Dr. Goebbels's thoughts are senseless demagoguery. "Poor Yorick!" is all you can say. He is a fellow of infinite jest and most excellent fancy, beginning with the popular attack on the Jews on November 9, 1938, the day of Germany's deepest shame,[114] and continuing through to the liquidation of Europe's Jews with bullets and gas, an act that *we* are now suffering for in bloody fashion. These two fancies alone are enough to secure him a place in Germany's cultural hall of fame.

Today, I flipped through the calendar looking for German days of commemoration that should be marked because they're in danger of not being included in next year's calendar. The pinnacle of these lapses in taste—January 24, 1712, and 1932: "Frederick the Great born, Herbert Norkus murdered"—demonstrates the absolute lack of any sense of *proportion* among our leaders.[115] Dr.Goebbels, too, fits in snugly between the signing of the Treaty of Westphalia and Luther's theses. Goebbels and his Führer have managed or will soon have managed to ensure that we receive a peace treaty that will put the Treaty of Westphalia to shame.

This much can be gleaned by the declaration of our three enemies from Yalta. The German Reich will be broken up to the extent that we will be *fully* neutralized as a center of power and no doubt split into many small parts. This is an issue completely separate from whether greater or lesser numbers of "high-placed" Germans are liquidated as we liquidated Jews. This is only a side matter that we brought on ourselves by spilling blood.

Perhaps I will be liquidated as an exponent of National Socialist tyranny and the rule of blood, who knows? No one will ask me whether I approved of all the terrible things or perhaps took part in them. That is what is so *infamous* about the measures we've taken. They involved the entire people in collective complicity and we cannot complain if our enemies say: You liquidated Jews with bullets and gas for ideological reasons and under the pretense of preserving world peace—now we are allowing ourselves the right to liquidate *you* for ideological reasons and under the pretense of preserving world peace.

Tübingen
February 23, 1945

Yesterday and today as of 9:30 A.M., there have been constant alarms. It's next to impossible to work because we're still under obsolete orders to take refuge in the cellars and take our typewriters along. That's why yesterday, I left the court and simply took my files back home. I had to wait for a long time in front of the inn before I entered with the first surge. Hardly were we inside after the all-clear was given, when another alarm sounded and everyone had to leave again! I finally ate at 3 o'clock. And the people put up with this life without complaining, like innocent little lambs! *Truly,* those currently in power could hardly have found more docile subjects. The people are happy as long as no bombs are dropped and they get some poor-quality, standard meal. It was the same story today, although I was lucky enough to be invited by the innkeepers for trout—a few of them still exist in Germany. When the food was on the table and we began our meal, which I celebrated like a holy mass, American bombers thundered without interruption over Tübingen. It was only because I kept a calm head that we did not run to the cellar and let our trout get cold. The bombers were getting ready to land so we could afford to make what looked like a heroic gesture. I heard that 900 were counted.

You could observe an interesting phenomenon during all this. The mother of the woman who runs the inn is an old lady of more than 70. You would think that she would be the last one to flee to the cellar, but in fact she's the one who absolutely can't be kept above ground, who seems more than any of us to cling to a life that is mostly *behind* her! You can make similar observations in bunkers. Old women and men are the first to want in and the last to go out again—despite the fact that the bunkers in my area are actually quite horrible since they only have a single entrance. If this is covered in rubble, hundreds of people get buried alive. I *never* go into them. I stay in my room, leaving only when the first bomb falls. If it hits my house, that's destiny and you can't escape fate.

There have been significant movements in the east and the west! In particular the First and Third American armies in the west appear to have commenced a massive advance, which our soldiers are resisting ruggedly and bitterly. What other army would do this, given the current situation? You only have to look at the map to see how hopeless it all is. Yet as we learned from Major Sch., whom we visited today after reporting to the new general, there is another hot rumor going around about new weapons. And there are *still* Germans who put some stock in this. If National Socialism has achieved one thing in the cultural realm, it's the fact that a whole people has stopped thinking! Dr. Goebbels can be immensely proud of that.

Tübingen
February 26, 1945

I'm including the Führer's proclamation, which appeared in today's newspapers, without any further commentary. Nothing more needs to be said: We've given the Führer 100 headquarters, but he should never have been allowed to come to power! When he predicts that the tide will turn this year (why not next year or the one after that?), he should tell the people *how* in the hell he plans to bring this about. In light of the experiences we've had thus far, the simplest sort of logic tells you that slogans like "Resistance to the last man and woman" don't bring victory.

One thing would be interesting to know. Does he still believe in what he says and predicts? If so, he's insane!

Tübingen
February 28, 1945

Today, on the heels of the Führer's proclamation, Dr. Goebbels was also heard from. He talked about the current situation. If clever formulations could win a war, we'd already be at the Ural Mountains! He spoke of coming victory, but just like the Führer, he was silent as to how this was to be achieved. At the same time, a report came over the radio that rations were being drastically reduced—down to 1,000 grams of bread and 125 grams of butter for the next period, which has already been pushed back by a week.

Goebbels did reassure us that the enemy would never take either himself or the rest of the leadership alive, which is small consolation for 80 million Germans who have been so badly deceived. We should remind him of this promise when the time comes, should *we* still be alive, which is doubtful.

It's a very bad sign that the leadership has to issue such reassurances to a confused and frightened people, of whom Goebbels once proclaimed that he needed a lantern to find anyone who did not believe in victory. Blowhard phrases of this sort come up utterly wanting when measured against fearsome reality. In the west, the enemy will soon reach the Rhine everywhere from Klewe to Cologne, and the English Second Army, which according to today's newspaper has remained idle near Venlo, hasn't even gotten involved in the fighting yet. Of course, if we bitterly defend every city, their advance will take time, but for how long will we continue to defend every city as bitterly as we've done so far?

I'm including Goebbels's speech as well, although it will soon only attract interest as a museum exhibit.

What nerve this man has! How dare he talk about gruesome maltreatment of women and children, when we've summarily murdered hundreds of thousands of Jewish women and children in Poland and Russia!

He talks about driving hundreds of Russian divisions out of the Reich. How? With words or with the poor *Volkssturm* or with divisions that we badly need but no longer have at our disposal? He repeats the phrases of Frederick the Great, who would roll over in his grave if he knew he were being compared to a lunatic dilettante who has led us to the brink of catastrophe.

It would be really interesting to know how many Germans recognize that this speech is utter nonsense and how many, even now, are still fooled by it.

Tübingen
March 1, 1944

Today I witnessed the strangest autopsy of my entire military service. An officer and chemist, on leave for further education, followed his wife, who had been left homeless by Allied bombing, in committing suicide. In and of itself, that is nothing special. What was special about the suicide was how carefully, indeed almost scientifically it was carried out. The man poisoned himself with cyanide, the formula for which he wrote out on his suicide note. The reverse side of the note contained the following:

1:13 P.M. CIGARETTE, 1:16 P.M. I INGEST THE POISON.

The man recorded a sticky sensation on the tongue, a raised pulse, dizziness, thirst, and then his words become illegible. Death must have come incredibly quickly. The note lay on his body, which in turn lay on the body of his wife. On a table there were letters to surviving family members and his last will and testament. On a commode directly next to the bed, there was a silver spoon with some sugary white powder in it.

The couple looked like wax sculptures and my secretary, who had never seen a corpse before, had to swallow hard. Still, the dictation was so objective and sober that it took away the terrible aspect of the situation for someone who isn't accustomed to scenes like this. The fact was: this couple made such an impression of rationally reflected calm that it was the behavior of their neighbors, whose daily routines had been interrupted and disturbed in this unusual fashion, which seemed truly painful. To my eyes they looked like two happy people who had put an intolerable burden behind them. But I'm old and my secretary is young. She's got a lot more to look forward to in life.

Today, it was impossible to get a lick of work done because of the constant alarms. And we're quite some distance from the front. It makes you ask: how are things going in the areas further west?

My wife, who's found quarters in Stockach ahead of being resettled in Krauchenwies, wrote that even in that miserable tiny town, bombs meant for the local train station fell near to where she is living and destroyed a number of houses. And Stockach is located on an ancillary line that is practically without significance. Hopefully they'll leave Krauchenwies, also located along this line near Sigmaringen, in peace.

We—that is, my division—will be moving on soon, but our destination hasn't been determined. There was talk most recently of Sigmaringen. Despite the French, there's meant to be room for us there. For me that would be an ideal solution because it's so near to Krauchenwies. I could go there quite often. With a "good" train connection, I might even be able to live there.

But regardless of where one is or goes, one can't escape the lost war. It may be preferable to live in a small town or village rather than a big city because it's easier to get supplies in the former. But there will be chaos and destruction there too, if the fighting continues until Germany is completely occupied. It will get more and more blackly comic to hear talk about final victory when half of Germany has been taken by the enemy. Our leadership can't behave any other way! But perhaps, if they don't dare to blather on about final victory and the turn of the tide any more, they'll level with the people and tell them they are supposed to die just like their glorious leadership. As utterly shameless as they are, our leaders indeed seem to be demanding precisely this from the people. And the people themselves? It is the most naive mass ever to populate a continent. Even *today* there are many who say that the Führer *must* have something up his sleeve or else he surely wouldn't dare to predict victory. God knows, our leaders have picked the right people to match their brand of politics.

Tübingen
March 5, 1945

Our front line to the west of the Rhine near Bonn has collapsed. That's a fact no one can deny. Our beaten troops are withdrawing to this side of the Rhine and the official line will be that this river of destiny will be the thing to finally stop our enemies—that is until this line, too, is crossed.

Signs that our economy is in its death throes are already evident in Tübingen despite calm in the city. Bakers are shutting up shop and it's getting harder and harder to secure the necessities. And this is just the beginning. Even Comrade G., an ardent National Socialist, is now of the opinion—one held by his wife for quite some time—that the war is lost. It took him a long time to admit this. But he's forced to go hungry, as am I, and that seems to have worn him down. I told him today that the difference between us was that he as a National Socialist has to *thank* our leadership for putting us where we are today whereas I, who was only a good German and not a National Socialist, am entitled to curse them, which brings with it a certain feeling of relief. He just gave me a bitter-sweet smile and said nothing.

Joking aside, it *is* like that. The fools who have led us to this catastrophe demand constant displays of respect toward our leadership. Can there be anything more insane than that? It would be one thing if they would admit that they hadn't had the luckiest of hands and demanded we respect their good intentions. But these arrogant dilettantes who thought they could conquer the world because they deceived themselves so utterly about the might of other countries simply demand respect, gratitude, and loyalty to the bitter end! Every newspaper article and every announcement is published for today and today only. Tomorrow fresh defeats will already render them obsolete. Still they feel no shame even though they remember *today* what they wrote *yesterday.* Today at court, while flipping through an edition of *Schwarzes Korps* from early January 1945, I found an article stating unequivocally that the Rundstedt Offensive would preclude *any* enemy advances and that *we* would emerge from this period under enemy pressure stronger for our having regrouped and improved our weapons and other matériel. I wish the author had been sitting in front of me—although I wouldn't be allowed to beat him over the head with the newspaper. That would be considered an enemy act of undermining our defensive morale.

It's tempting to make more predictions. How long will the war last and how will it end? Will our troops continue to fight until Germany has been completely conquered and occupied? Will they resign themselves to their fate and quit fighting so that the enemy can make speedy breakthroughs or will they mutiny and bash in their commanding officers' skulls? Those are the three possibilities for the future. The second and third scenarios could coincide, if the officer corps, with its diminishing power, tries to force troops to continue the fight. I simply *cannot* imagine that there will be an organized resistance in the rest of the German territories if the Ruhr and Saar valleys and the Palatinate have been conquered to the west, and Berlin and Saxony have fallen to the east. And that will come. On the other hand, our enemies will have to take these two bulwarks before we will collapse and that could entail a number of weeks.

It's possible that we may have an English landing on the North Sea coastline to reckon with. It's striking how few troops England has deployed in the west. As far as I understand, there are two English armies there and one of those is actually Canadian. England has 48 million inhabitants and surely several million soldiers so that they would have several armies available for deployment. Perhaps they're just waiting for the other troops to force a battle on the Rhine, tying down all German forces there, before launching a landing. In *that* case it would surely be a stunning success! But perhaps they lack the shipping capacities, which are needed right now to supply the armies on the western front.

Qui vivra verra.

Tübingen
March 12, 1945

Nothing special on the fronts except that the American, which I didn't think he would manage, has succeeded in crossing the Rhine near Remagen and establishing a bridgehead. It can only be held, of course, because the US Air Force can stop major attacks by bombing concentrations of troops and transport axes. Otherwise a lone bridgehead wouldn't survive long—we have enough troops to push it back. This bridgehead shows how confident our enemies feel. If they had made crossings at four to six locations, with one of two divisions per crossing, it would not have been nearly as daring as it seems right now.

In the east pressure is growing on Danzig. The city's days—or perhaps weeks—are numbered. The Stettin Lagoon is under the same sort of pressure. The major central offensive against Berlin and Saxony hasn't begun yet. It will cause General Dittmar to claim that the front has been stabilized to an extent. The stabilization, however, is that our enemies can make intensive preparations without being bothered in the slightest by us. Every time there's a pause in the fighting, you hear foolish talk about stabilization. But what else can the sort of people who work in the Propaganda Ministry say?

I'm including the Führer's proclamation. He intends to keep on fighting until the others have had enough or Germany is occupied—the latter being the more probable scenario since it seems hardly likely the others will have had enough any time soon. The Führer did not dare, however, to elucidate what occupation would entail!

It's grotesque. When [Philippe] Pétain, faced with a hopeless situation like ours is now, capitulated, he was hailed as a man with the highest sense of responsibility. By contrast, [Paul] Reynaud, who behaved as our leadership is trying to, was cursed all the way to hell and back as a shameless slaughterer of his own people for suggesting that France sacrifice a single *poilu* [French infantryman] for a lost cause.[116]

In Germany, the same thing is not condemned as irresponsibility. It's held up as a demonstration of highest sense of national duty toward the people who, as the reasoning goes, would otherwise be annihilated. As if they will *not* be annihilated if the fighting continues.

All of this demonstrates the internal dishonesty of our regime, which from an ethical standpoint richly deserves to fail in every one of its endeavors. In an ethical sense, there is not a single true word spoken any more. The truth *has* to be banned or else the state will implode.

My wife and Benno write from Krauchenwies that food is very *scarce*. We've been discussing by letter whether they should return to Freiburg, although they only left a short while ago.

The reason is simple. There are still a hundred pounds of potatoes in our cellar that one could gradually remove in a rucksack. They wouldn't have to starve—that is what this means, no more and no less. But people will be starving in this country if the war proceeds slowly.

It seems to me that in the short term all means available are being used to occupy the north so that our enemies will meet up somewhere in central Germany, north of the Main River. They'll *only* move on southern Germany when the *north* has been occupied and they wouldn't expect to encounter serious resistance. In this case, the enemy's attack and breakthrough would come from the north and through Alsace to the west, and perhaps it would happen so quickly that large-scale evacuations would no longer be possible. Evacuations, you see, are what will cause starvation—together with the breakdown of the transportation system, which has already started.

If Freiburg is overrun, it would be preferable to be there and put the war behind us. I, however, will be separated from my family for the foreseeable future until an armistice is reached. I'll have to accept this. Daisy and Benno's lives are more important than my own.

What indescribable suffering our unhappy leadership has brought upon Germany! We three—bombed out, impoverished, homeless, and without bed, kitchen, and apartment—are just a small part of the millions of people who are doing equally badly and whose fate doesn't move our genius of a Führer in the slightest. It would move him if he were required to throw himself into battle, where he belongs, or upon his sword instead of waiting until all Germany shares our fate. But some higher power seems to demand that we face this test perhaps because once destruction has come to Germany, the idea of National Socialism will be eradicated once and for all and will only call forth horror and vows of "Never again!"

After this war, how opinions will diverge! Those who supported our quest for power will internally distance themselves since everything that reminds us of this quest for power, first and foremost the military, will be utterly uprooted and discarded. That is *fully* inconceivable to Germans right now, but it's inevitable. The officer corps is facing a final twilight more terrible than any they could have imagined. The important thing, though, is for everyone to recognize that this is a consequence of our unbelievably dilettantish political leadership! If the people acknowledge *this,* they will be saved at least internally. If not, they will be hopelessly lost. Some people say that Hitler and his vassals are the only ones who want to continue the war. They're surely wrong. The entire active officer corps must have an interest in continuing to fight since in an economic sense, final defeat would take away the basis of their existence. There won't be any pensions for generals between 40 and 50 years of age.[117]

No matter how hard one tries to look toward the future and forget about oneself, things are dark, very dark indeed.

Tübingen
March 22, 1945

I just listened to a radio broadcast of Hitler Youth songs, quite nicely sung. Our leadership is, as I've remarked before, a leadership of "as if," a leadership that acts as if the front had not collapsed and everything were still just fine. For an alert observer, this creates a gruesome contrast between illusion and reality. If our leadership had restricted itself to composing the words and music of patriotic songs, the contrast would have been absolutely tragicomic. That [the cultural wing] is a part of the organization, its uppermost floor, so to speak. Further down come the executioners, Gestapo, and murderers of Jews who eradicate everything the idealists have created and composed. *This*, however, is the German problem postwar Germany will have to confront. Is such a regime tolerable from a human and ethical standpoint? Anyone who thinks it is tolerable, despite the terrible crimes of which it was culpable, can play no role in the renewal of German life. Opinions differ here, but there is no room for concession because that would be the worst sort of hypocrisy, very un-German. The famous English saying "my country, right or wrong"[118] cannot extend this far. Dr. Goebbels may want it to, but I don't believe that the core of our people has been so corrupted that they will simply shrug their shoulders at our massive guilt and carry on as before. *I* know *no one* who fails to condemn these terrible things when engaged in serious conversation.

Externally, one is of course hampered by fear and keeps one's mouth shut.

Events are proceeding at a tumultuous pace along the western front. The American has broken through over the lower Mosel River and has advanced along the Rhine via Bingen and Worms into the Ludwigshafen area. Our army in the Saarland, if it even still exists as an army, has ceded ground and is in danger of being fully cut off. Very soon we'll have lost both the Saar region and the Palatinate and then our enemies will cross the Rhine, in many locations, I think, from Wesel to Bonn and later to the south of the bridgehead at Remagen. At the same time, the Russian will commence a large-scale action in the center. He may not force the issue in Berlin. He may besiege the city and starve it into submission, which surely wouldn't take very long. I fear that the result of these invasions will be that the Russian and Anglo-American armies will join up somewhere in central Germany.

Germans often seem capable of anything, but in *that* case, it will be highly doubtful that our propaganda will be to keep up its triumphant wailing and infuse people with hope.

Yesterday a ministerial order was circulated. It prohibits German soldiers from plundering in liberated areas and concludes by stating that the Russian will soon be driven from eastern Germany. That's what our leadership has decided anyway.

Alas, Herr Himmler, if such paper decisions could change anything, the situation would already be different. Where are we supposed to get the hundreds of divisions we need to make this happen?

I'm very anxious to see precisely when our leadership's boastful posturing will cease. When all northern Germany is occupied? Or will they try to convince the people they're about to grab the enemy by the collar and throw him out?

Tübingen
March 23, 1945

Today at 6:30 A.M. (to avoid being interrupted by alarms), a senior officer lectured us about the situation. Before I forget it, I want to record the essence of what he said. It was as follows:

1. There was no need to make many remarks about the seriousness of our situation.
2. The necessary troops had been allocated to begin an offensive to the east and drive off the Russians.
3. That necessarily meant our western armies would be weakened to an extent.
4. The potential on the left bank of the Rhine could not be contained so that all our troops had to withdraw over the river.
5. The bridgehead in Remagen made it necessary to deploy new troops to prevent this "tumor" from growing, given that eight American divisions had already crossed over.

6. For this reason, the eastern offensive had yet to commence, so that Pomerania had been lost.

7. If the bridge in R. had been destroyed promptly, we would have been in a position to defend the Rhine for *months* and the eastern offensive would already be underway.

8. The fighter program has been discontinued. If the fighters had been deployed, the result would have been massive air battles. Deploying only some of the fighters would have been inopportune since it would have only led to the enemy deploying his entire airborne forces, instead of just parts of them, and would have increased the destruction.

9. If I understood correctly, the new weapons were ready for use.

10. He could not say when they would be used, only *that* they would be.

Everything else he said we just the same old political clichés we read every day in the newspapers. What struck me were the following slips:

1. We should beware of underestimating our enemy and his leadership and calling Churchill a whiskey drunk. The good man apparently forgot that the Führer used precisely this formulation.

2. We underestimated the potential of our enemies, particularly the Russians, to arm themselves by not a hundredfold, but a thousandfold. Does the good man

know what he's saying? If that was so, was it necessary to attack the Russians? Does this statement not show that we attacked Russia because we thought it would be easily beatable and not because we feared the Russians would attack us?

One could say here: *quod licet Jovi, non licet bovi*.[119] If one of our kind said these sorts of things and someone reported him, he could be *sure* he'd be brought up before a military court for criticizing the Führer. So much for this lecture. The coming weeks will show whether it was anything more than mere fairy tales.

But I forget something.

Submarine warfare, the senior officer told us, is now being restarted. Previous announcements to that effect were an attempt to confuse the enemy abroad and thus had to be made at home as well. It's good to record such things while they're fresh in your memory. By the way it occurred to me that the bridgehead at Remagen might serve as the starting point for a stab-in-the-back legend. Perhaps we'll hear more about that later on, if things go badly. It's a very modest story for a stab-in-the-back legend. Still it's one that could be used.

Tübingen
March 24, 1945

Our propaganda officer gave a public speech. I'm including an excerpt. He didn't dare tell us what the newspapers are writing, namely that the words of our Führer promising that the historic turning point would come this year are to be regarded as *gospel*. What blasphemy! This lecture revealed the true nature of our propaganda. Nothing but promises that can't be kept, empty phrases, and threats. There's nothing left to say about it.

Tübingen
March 28, 1945

One year ago today, I began recording my thoughts. Perhaps after the war they will not be completely uninteresting since they are a candid attempt to do justice to reality and to break free from the empty phrases of propaganda.

Everything I feared then has come true. Sometimes, before the collapse of the eastern front, I thought we would be caught in a stranglehold deep into the year 1945, but in the wake of our final twilight in the east, there can be no more talk of that. Still, a few months ago, I would never have through that our complete collapse would come so quickly and in such giant steps this spring.

Everywhere in the west, it's crazy. Our enemies have crossed over the Rhine from Wesel to Ludwigshafen, and there are no larger holes in their lines. Their tanks are rolling through Germany just as our tanks rolled through France in 1940.

It is clear that organized resistance in the hinterlands will be impossible. Here and there there's a replacement army or a battalion or a company, dispersed through towns large and small, but the replacement troops have been so thoroughly combed for battle-ready men that such replacement divisions don't really possess any fighting strength.

With us, the situation is that we are just about able to provide 8,000 men for a brigade charged with "shielding" the area from Karlsruhe toward Heilbronn. A brigade like this will simply be blown away by the enemy with his tanks and air might. Energetic fighters might be able to achieve temporary local triumphs, which the news would then blow all out of proportion so as to conceal the true situation. But any real large-scale resistance is unthinkable.

Where will such actions lead? We discuss this question a lot because we are all southern Germans and natives of Baden.

The southernmost crossing of the Rhine took place near Mannheim. South of there, all the way down to Basel, the enemy is at the Rhine and is capable of crossing it whenever he wants, assuming he's got the necessary numbers. On the right bank of the Rhine, in the Black Forest, are the remnants of the 19th Army, which fought their way back across the river. The question is now whether the enemy plans to conquer northern and central Germany, meet up with the Russians somewhere west of Berlin and then push down south—which he'll be able to do pretty much without a fight if he's already taken care of northern and central Germany. Or perhaps he'll cross the Rhine at Karlsruhe and push down south on the right bank of the river, bypassing the Black Forest to his left. Or perhaps he'll combine such an action with crossings at various locations.

I believe he'll choose the first strategic option because it would come at the smallest cost. There would be no real line of resistance against the overpowering might of an enemy rolling down from the north. Any and all resistance would simply be crushed.

A further question, posed by a soldier: If northern and central Germany are over and done with, will we still have control over our troops, or do we not run the risk of mass mutiny and desertion?

All these questions will be answered soon—even though they are significant only for the destiny of individuals, but not for our collective destiny. The latter can no longer be changed. I think that northern and central Germany will be occupied within a few weeks. We're receiving orders from above [Himmler] about setting up drumhead courts-martial to suppress "instances of dissolution," as if in this the final act even the most brutal form of justice could help.[120] Our "harshest" judge, who was identified as such within the Corps Court in Stuttgart, has been appointed to head the drumhead court in Tübingen and is expected to set heads rolling for final victory! (I stand in good favor personally as a quick worker, but am considered far too lenient in executing my duties.) He's not to be envied. The job is unpleasant even for someone who is indeed too harsh and without any human feelings.

My mildness as a judge is probably the reason I wasn't promoted, but I'm proud of it. I have always considered it my job to intervene to *protect* soldiers who have slipped up and to prevent immoral, humiliating punishments. I think that I have, in my own way, served the collective well. I have rarely been disappointed in the soldiers whom I have helped wherever possible.

Perhaps when everything goes topsy-turvy, I will be shot to death by an unknown, anonymous soldier who regards me as the source of all evil. I couldn't change that, if it should be the case.[121]

Tübingen
March 30, 1945

The army report is devastating. Gdynia and Danzig have been lost, East Prussia has collapsed amidst funeral dirges about heroic battle, the Russian is on the Austrian border, the Englishman and American have advanced deep into Germany with armies of tanks, and we have nothing to counter them. Yet still the fighting continues! The fighting continues although the most dim-witted, optimistic fool couldn't possibly believe that our fortunes will turn around. The fighting continues because gentlemen on high refuse to sacrifice themselves and are trying to save their own necks for a few months, even at the great risk of mass starvation. But what does our irresponsible leadership care about the people, the long-suffering people who will put up with anything? They are just cannon fodder in the struggle to extend a hopeless battle.

In light of such Wehrmacht reports and the even worse ones sure to follow, what impertinence it takes to demand that people fight on! But the moment will come, when the troops realize that the battle is senseless and refuse to fight, and this moment will come sooner than our leaders, who are so fearful for their lives, would like.

Tübingen

March 31, 1945

In Tübingen, people are building antitank barricades in the streets and on the bridge over the Neckar River. I can't imagine anything more laughable than this gesture of the district Nazi leader who will have *long* absconded by the time the tanks roll in. The soldiers watch such dilettantism and grin, thinking, no doubt, private thoughts in their heads.

My prognosis is that if, as it appears, northern and central Germany are subdued militarily and armies of tanks press on in a broad front toward the south, hardly a shot will be fired! How many battle-ready troops do we have? There are replacement battalions and companies of convalescents, but they're dispersed everywhere. I presume that our division has already handed over all its men (3,000) who are fit for battle. Anyone left isn't battle worthy and no command will change that fact. For that reason I think the fears of many Tübingen natives, panicked at the thought of street fighting, are completely unfounded. The district party leader's dismay can be dismissed as a fantasy especially considering that the coward no doubt has aimed this gesture more at above than at below.

Tübingen
April 1, 1945

Easter Sunday was rung in in the early hours by fighter bombers who dropped their payloads near the city. I was shaving at the time. Otherwise, nothing has happened today.

This evening, a "proclamation" of the liberation movement "Werewolf" was read out over the radio. The movement was formed in the occupied west or—in my opinion—in the Propaganda Ministry in Berlin. It threatens enemy soldiers with all sorts of terrorist reprisals. I'm including it here, just as it appeared.

If this phenomenon is serious, it is an act of criminal insanity by young activists who do not know what they are doing or how much force the enemy has at his disposal. If he wants to stop the movement quickly, he need only deport the local youth everywhere terrorist acts occur—assuming he doesn't opt for more drastic measures like absolutely leveling those places with bombs.

In point of fact, the idea for the movement came from Dr. Goebbels. Here too posters have been put up threatening the English with hanging under the slogan, "werewolves

sink their claws in." And the authorities and the police tolerate this—for lack of a better word—nonsense.

Tübingen
April 4, 1945

Today 14-year-old Hitler Youths arrived here. They have
been taken from their parents in Heidelberg and are now
supposed to act as "werewolves." Fourteen-year-old boys! A
graver crime is hardly imaginable. Those who pull the strings
are sitting in complete safety in the south and these boys
are supposed to sacrifice themselves. It can only be hoped
that this infernal plan fails. Nonetheless, it's inconceivable
how parents can let their children go, especially now that
the power of the party apparatus is increasingly waning and
punishment—except for a trumped-up court run by werewolves themselves—is out of the question.

Well done! Nothing reveals the system of the Third Reich
to be so thoroughly rotten and immoral as such actions. I
believe that Providence did not allow the putsch of July 20
to succeed because it would otherwise have become a stab-
in-the-back legend that would have divided the people for
years. Half of Germany would surely have fallen for this
myth, creating a fatal rupture.

The rupture is no longer possible. *No* stab-in-the-back
legend, no matter what may be invented at the last minute,
will have power to persuade. The people *have* to endure
the ultimate misery of this lost war so that the last and

stupidest German also says: Never again National Socialism. For that reason, all these mechanisms of desperation,
even those as shameless and immoral as the misuse of these
Hitler Youths, are necessary. They serve to open Germany's
eyes.

Bombs fell again today on the Hindenburg barracks.
They came at the time when the general usually gives his
address. But he's in Münsingen and we weren't required to
fall out. That's why we're still alive. If the fighter bombers
struck quickly, there would have been large numbers of dead
and seriously injured. I watched the attack from my window.
The panes rattled but held. It is crazy how one gets used to
things. One doesn't seek shelter in the cellar anymore because it's senseless to sit around there for hours with nothing
to do but wait and see if anything happens.

Tübingen
April 6, 1945

I just finished listening to one the usual reports about our
situation that pretended that we were still capable of meaningful resistance and blathered on about ultimate victory.
Fewer and fewer radio stations, though, are broadcasting
this idiocy. I've heard the Stuttgart station is off the air. All
the city's civil servants have fled, with the gauleiter and district leaders leading the way. They did this on exactly the
same day that Himmler ordered them to stay, fight, and die.
They didn't want to do that, these gentlemen who have led

a life of luxury for the past 12 years and don't want to give it up.

The offices in Ludwigsburg seem to be empty too. An inspector told of how the court of the commander of POWs shipped out as the final unit and arrived here in search of a "place to stay." The deputy general commando is said to have moved to Ravensburg. How long do they plan to stay there?

We, too, are "taking off": The advance commando is leaving tonight, and the rest will follow them next week to Saulgau. Here, too, you could ask: For how long?

The front, which is no longer a front even in name, can no longer be held. Our division with its replacement battalions has no fighting power whatsoever after being forced to hand over all of our battle-fit men.

If I didn't have a wife and child, it would be fascinating to follow the complete dissolution of a state unique in that it calls upon every form of public violence, not just the military in and of itself. But my situation is different. I have Daisy and Benno in Krauchenwies and I am duty-bound to care for them. Normally, I would accept only death or captivity unless the staff and troops gradually agreed to dissolve and demobilize.

Now when I am given files about men going AWOL, 80 percent of the time it's impossible to pursue them since the men are in a battle zone or somewhere that will soon be a battle zone and where we can't get messages to. Here, too, we are witnessing all the signs of dissolution and collapse.

Today I was supposed to hear five cases. But neither a single defendant nor witness was able to appear.

Tübingen
April 8, 1945

The day before yesterday, in the evening, the division staff left for Saulgau without notifying us—to say nothing of issuing us any orders. As a result we're sitting here waiting for the truck to return from Saulgau and pick us up. But as I heard from an officer of the follow-up commando, the truck apparently had gotten stuck or broken down somewhere. It's supposed to have left Saulgau yesterday afternoon. But it still hasn't arrived here.

Thus, this morning, before the news of the breakdown arrived, we sat around court waiting. The court of the commander of POWs from Ludwigsburg, who wanted to go "somewhere," is also quartering with us. The head of the court, the general of the POWs, has already gone ahead, somewhere south, in a car.

These are all signs that the dissolution of the regular army is well underway.

Unfortunately, today saw some intense aerial bombing, and we heard gigantic detonations to the south of Tübingen. That will no doubt have once more cut rail traffic to Sigmaringen. It appears extremely unlikely that we'll be moving out by rail.

We'll have to find another truck so that we can ship out. It would almost be amusing if the enemy were to advance south through Stuttgart, which would be no great problem, and "introduce himself" here. Anything is possible. It's reminiscent of conditions in France in 1940.

There, though, a man with a sense of responsibility appeared and put an end to the insanity of hopeless resistance. Our newspapers praised him as a responsible statesman while they called Reynaud an abomination for wanting to continue the French resistance. *Here,* we are terrorized by a lunatic who wants to save the necks of himself and his buddies for a few more months.

That's the only difference between France in 1940 and Germany in 1945.

Poor, poor Germany! If our leadership clique had even the slightest sense of responsibility toward the people, they would have abdicated—since they are unwilling to [take responsibility and] capitulate. But these criminals, who are now revealing themselves for what they are, don't think for a moment of sparing the people further sacrifice and misery. The small criminal gang, which has sacrificed millions of upstanding German soldiers, cannot decide to sacrifice their own miserable lives.

In 1933 the upright and naive German people granted this leadership more leeway than has ever been given to a government in human history. And now all we have is the ruins of a leadership that was as criminal as it was dilettantish. How many Germans *today* are unable to see clearly through the fog of propaganda?

It's terrible that we are losing the war. But assuming I live to see it, which is questionable, I shall praise the day when the radio and the newspapers stop spewing out their mendacious clichés. The day when one is allowed to hear and speak honest words again, or to live without fear that some lowlife informer will turn you in for a slightly too frank phrase. Those are immaterial things that cannot be held in high enough regard. For a man who loves the truth and possesses a sense of justice, it will be akin to salvation to no longer have to listen to General Dittmar or be force-fed Dr. Goebbels's Jesuit articles.

What I find most shattering about the case of Dittmar, who is after all a general and not a party bigwig, is his utter lack of shame. Every day for years, he gave lectures about our victory and he shows no remorse! If he had even the smallest remainder of shame, honor, and bearing, he would have discontinued those lectures. Why doesn't he do this? Is he paid that well? Was he afraid of being liquidated if he declared that he could no longer square this with his conscience as an upstanding soldier? He *isn't* an upstanding soldier anymore. The regime has removed his spine, just as it did to the people!

Wolfurt[122]

April 21, 1945

"And further to the east it went / With steps of storm and fight / The little rod in the midst were we / Of Frenchmen to the left and right!" The worst thing was that we kept getting

Diary entry of April 21, 1945

further and further away from our homeland. Finally, we ended up beyond Bregenz in Wolfurt. There we disbanded.

You were now a civilian and had to try to get through without being put in a POW camp. My lucky star spared me that fate, although I reported to the command.

It was now a matter of obtaining the laissez-passer to Freiburg. That required countless trips to Bregenz.

Wolfurt
April 30, 1945

There seems to be almost no prospect of leaving here legally. I'm planning a "break-out" on foot with a knapsack full of the most important things for the house and some preserved food. At the mayor's office, I looked through the map. I have to try to get beyond Pfänder Mountain and reach Baden-Bavarian soil. But that's no easy task. Among the military judges, only one—the fanatic Nazi Ge.—is still here.

Around six weeks ago, he began to curse Hitler and the whole party pigsty. Perhaps it was in order to lay the groundwork for a clean bill of political health later. He may be able to get away with it when, as is sure to come, his past comes in for closer examination. After all he was only a silly Nazi and we were usually able to overturn his bloodthirsty sentences. What's amazing is that he has already received his laissez-passer. Probably that's because he's suffering from a ruptured hernia.

Wolfurt
May 20, 1945

I'm still here and slowly beginning to lose faith. My days consist of going for a walk, then eating a little something, and then planning how I might get through. If I were a civilian, it wouldn't be dangerous to be caught without a laissez-passer. But as a discharged staff judge, the price of such an enterprise would be internment in a POW camp.

Wolfurt
June 5, 1945

The Commander's Office of Bregenz be praised. It issued me the laissez-passer and as soon as possible, I'll be setting off.

Wolfurt
June 7, 1945

I paid one last visit to the nice farmer in the mountains above W. He was a humane man who always gave me milk and bread. In return, the supply of cigarettes with which I thanked him grew ever smaller. On my last visit, I took along a knapsack which for the purpose of physical exercise I'd filled with stones. It was then that I had my final confrontation with the victorious French army.

I walked up a path through the woods and encountered French patrol, a noncommissioned officer with two common foot soldiers, who immediately indicated for me to stop. "Vos papiers!" (Your papers!)

I handed them over for inspection, took the heavy knapsack from my shoulders and placed it on the ground.

The NCO kicked at it and asked: "Qu'est ça que vous avez dans le sac?" (What do you have in your knapsack?)

The Müller-Hills in the late 1960s on the balcony of their apartment in the Herdern neighborhood of Freiburg, where Müller-Hill's wife and child took shelter during the Allied air raid in 1944.

For the first time I felt totally superior to the victor, although also very nervous and agitated: "Rien d'intéressant pour vous." (Nothing that would interest you.)

The NCO picked up the rucksack, weighed it in his hand, and looked at me sharply: "Ouvrez." (Open it!)

I replied: "Mais je vous ai dit que ce n'est pas intéressant pour vous." (But I said it was nothing that would interest you.)

The NCO: "Ouvrez." (Open it!)

I opened the knapsack, which contained nothing but stones. The NCO was speechless: "Des pierres." (Stones!)

The footsoldiers: "Des pierres." (Stones!)

The NCO: "Passez." (You may pass.)

Over my shoulder I heard him say to the foot soldiers: "Complètement fou." (Completely crazy.)

NOTES

Introduction

1. "Der laute Kamerad," *Der Spiegel,* February 9, 1955, 16.
2. Joachim Perels, "Die Ausschaltung des Justizapparats der NS-Diktatur—Voraussetzung der demokratischen Neubeginns," in *Mit reinem Gewissen: Wehrmachtrichter in der Bundesrepublik und ihre Opfer,* edited by Joachim Perels and Wolfram Wette (Berlin: Aufbau Verlag, 2011), 22; Peter Kalmbach, *Wehrmachtjustiz* (Berlin: Metropol Verlag, 2012), 13; detailed discussion of numbers in Manfred Messerschmidt and Fritz Wüllner, *Die Wehrmachtjustiz im Dienst des Nationalsozialismus: Zerstöring einer Legende* (Baden-Baden: Nomos Verlagsgesellschaft, 1987), 63–89.
3. Wolfram Wette, "Frühe Selbstentlastung der Wehrmachtrichter—späte Rehabilitierung ihrer Opfer," in Perels and Wette, *Mit reinem Gewissen,* 83.
4. All biographical facts are from the introduction to the German edition of this book: Wolfram Wette, "Kein Blutrichter. Die Aufzeichungen des untypischen Wehrmachtsjuristen Werner Otto Müller-Hill," in *"Man hat es kommen sehen und ist doch erschüttert." Das Kriegstagebuch eines deutschen Heeresrichters 1944/45* (Munich: Siedler Verlag, 2012), 9–10.
5. Messerschmidt and Wüllner, *Die Wehrmachtjustiz im Dienst des Nationalsozialismus,* 38–41.
6. Ibid., 51, 90, 133.
7. Diary, April 19, 1944.
8. A particularly thought-provoking example of the last of these is Dagmar Herzog, *Sex after Fascism: Memory and Morality in Twentieth-Century Germany* (Princeton, NJ: Princeton University Press, 2005). On Goebbels see Peter Longerich, *Goebbels: Biographie* (Munich: Siedler Verlag, 2010).
9. See Nathan Stoltzfus, *Resistance of the Heart: Intermarriage and the Rosenstrasse Protest in Nazi Germany* (New Brunswick, NJ: Rutgers University Press, 2001); Saul Friedländer, *Nazi Germany and the Jews,* vol. 1: *The Years of Persecution 1933–1939* (New York:

HarperCollins, 1997); vol. 2: *The Years of Extermination 1939–1945* (New York: HarperCollins, 2008).

10. Grete Dölker-Rehder, diary, quoted in Walter Kempowski, *Das Echolot: Barbarossa '41. Ein kollektives Tagebuch* (Munich: Albrecht Knaus Verlag, 2002), 53, 70, 117; Theodore S. Hamerow, *On the Road to the Wolf's Lair: German Resistance to Hitler* (Cambridge, MA: Harvard University Press, 1999).

11. Kempowski, *Echelot;* Ian Kershaw, *The End: The Defiance and Destruction of Hitler's Germany, 1944–1945* (New York: Penguin, 2011), 70, 132, 152–56.

12. Ian Kershaw, *Hitler, Germans, and the Final Solution* (New Haven, CT: Yale University Press, 2008), 199, 204; Ian Kershaw, *Popular Opinion and Political Dissent in the Third Reich: Bavaria 1933–1945* (New York: Oxford University Press, 2002), 277.

13. Diary, June 5, 1944.

14. Diary, March 29, 1944, January 27, 1945, April 5, 1944.

15. Diary, March 28, 1944, December 16, 1944, December 31, 1944, May 24, 1944.

16. Diary, March 28, 1945, April 11, 1944, February 3, 1945.

17. Diary, March 28, 1945, April 11, 1944.

18. Diary, October 20, 1944, October 16, 1944, October 22, 1944.

19. Diary, March 1, 1945.

20. Diary, March 12, 1945.

21. "Der laute Kamerad," *Der Spiegel,* February 9, 1955, 18.

22. Wolfram Wette, *The Wehrmacht: History, Myth, Reality* (Cambridge, MA: Harvard University Press, 2007); Joachim Perels, "Die Ausschaltung des Justizapparats der NS-Diktatur—Voraussetzung der demokratischen Neubeginns," in Perels and Wette, *Mit reinem Gewissen,* 35–36; Jacqueline Roussety, "Der Politiker Hans K. Filbinger und der Soldat Walter Gröger: Ein Essay," in ibid.,101–102; Perels and Wette "Einleitung," in ibid., 19; Kalmbach, *Wehrmachtjustiz,* 284.

Journal Entries: March 28, 1944–June 7, 1945

1. The book referred to is Philipp Bouhler's *Napoleon: Kometenbahn eines Genies.* The author was the head of the Führer's Chancellery and was responsible for the Nazis' euthanasia program. His biography of Napoleon, published in 1941, was supposedly one of Hitler's favorite books. In it, Bouhler depicts Napoleon as one of the rare great men produced by history. But he also criticizes the French emperor, writing that Napoleon's struggle against England had to end in failure "because in the final phases of this battle he saw the unbelievably dynamic force of the German people rising up against him." His depiction of Napoleon, Bouhler argues in his preface, touches "on ideas that still move history in our day, the mission of our own people, and its task create a new permanent order in Europe." Bouhler thus understood his own depiction of Napoleon as a political-ideological introduction for world war.

2. H. refers to Hitler. It was common practice during and even after the Third Reich (see Golo Mann's *Deutsche Geschichte des 19. und 20.*

Jahrhunderts) not to write out the dictator's full name, perhaps because it was so associated with terror.

3. Romania fought as an ally of Nazi Germany against the Soviet Union from 1941 to late summer 1944, when the Red Army achieved a breakthrough. On August 23 of that year, the Romanian head of state Ion Antonescu was arrested and later executed. On August 25, Romania declared war on Germany.

4. The so-called "V weapons"—the German word for "retribution" is *Vergeltung*—were also referred to in Goebbels's hypertrophic propaganda as "miracle weapons." The included the unmanned V-1 rocket and the long-distance V-2 ballistic missile. It was claimed that they would turn around the course of the war at the very last minute, ensuring "final victory" for Hitler and the Third Reich. The weapons failed to live up to expectations either psychologically or militarily, although they did kill thousands and wound tens of thousands in Belgium, particularly in Antwerp, where they were used most frequently.

5. Cassino, located 130 kilometers southeast of Rome in the province of Latium, was the site of one of the most protracted and bloodiest battles of World War II. The German leadership hoped to halt Allied advances there and succeeded in doing so for months. Poor weather, difficult terrain, supply problems, and the tactics employed by Colonel General Heinrich von Vietinghoff stymied British and American troops until mid-May 1944, when they were able to break through enemy lines at Montecassino.

     Kurt Dittmar (1891–1959) was a major general and a radio commentator who read out Wehrmacht reports.

6. All emphases are those of Müller-Hill in the original diary.

7. The city of Danzig/Gdansk played a major role in justifications of war in Nazi propaganda. The Treaty of Versailles had separated Danzig, whose population was 90 percent German, from the German Reich and declared it a free city under the protection of the League of Nations. In 1939 Hitler used the controversial status of the city as an instrument first to pressure and then, when Warsaw had predictably refused demands to return Danzig to the Reich, to declare war on Poland. On September 2, 1939, one day after Hitler ordered the Wehrmacht to attack Poland, Danzig was reintegrated into the German Reich. Nonetheless, its importance for German propaganda continued. After France had declared war on Germany, Nazi propaganda asked French soldiers: "Mourir pour Danzig?" (Are you willing to die for Danzig?) Still, the retaking of Danzig was more a pretense for Hitler to attack Poland than an end in and of itself.

8. *Gauleiter* were the Nazi Party's regional leaders and were usually quite fanatic.

9. The date Germany attacked the Soviet Union.

10. Hermann Keyserling's *Das Spektrum Europas* was published in Heidelberg in 1928. It is an essayistic travel journal in twelve chapters that describe, mock, and ironize various nations' national characters. Keyserling wrote, for instance, that the products of nationalism could only be correctly understood as symptoms of a disease. From his observations and experiences, the author draws three conclusions. First,

in no country does reality conform to the way people see themselves. Second, there is "no greater variety in the world than in Europe . . . not even in India despite the enormous color of that part of the globe." And third, "all of Europe is essentially of one mind and spirit."

11. This is a reference to events leading up to World War II: the March 1936 reoccupation of the Rhineland, which the treaties of Versailles and Locarno had demilitarized; the March 1938 *Anschluss* (attachment) of Austria to the Reich; and the September 1938 annexation of the Sudetenland section of Czechoslovakia with its large population of ethnic Germans as part of the Munich agreement. These "steps" freed Nazi Germany from most of the international restrictions binding it and gave the regime internal legitimacy.

12. The reference is to the reoccupation of the Rhineland. On March 7, 1936, Hitler sent German troops into the demilitarized area of western Germany in violation of the Treaty of Locarno. This was a massive gamble since the troops would not have had sufficient force to resist had they been attacked. France and Britain, however, were unable to agree on a response to this provocation and did essentially nothing, so Hitler was able to achieve his first "coup."

13. Because of their desires to keep the peace, England and France suffered from what cultural history professor Philipp Gassert has called a "self-blockade." Hitler had cleverly mollified English worries early on with a treaty concerning German fleet sizes, and French policies were primarily oriented toward self-defense. The West was also confronted with a number of foreign and internal problems, which helped distract attention from Hitler's expansionism.

14. Müller-Hill is referring to demands by the German leadership for "what the German people are rightfully due," that is, that all Germans live in a single state. The Nazi demands for the annexation of Sudetenland and the return of Danzig to the Reich were both subsumed under this larger principle.

15. Müller-Hill counts back the years since the 1936 reoccupation of the Rhineland.

16. Hitler realized his foreign-policy aims by breaking international agreements and treaties like the Treaty of Versailles, the Treaty of Locarno, and the Munich agreement. The lack of sanctions following these acts of bad faith convinced both him and the German public that they could defy the international community with impunity.

17. What is apparently meant is the battle against the West, the democratic-capitalist system and its supposed culture of decadence.

18. Fellahin were peasants in the Middle East and Northern Africa. See Oswald Spengler, *Der Untergang des Abendlandes* (English translation: *The Decline of the West*). Spengler attempted, in his own words, to "predetermine history" for the first time ever: in the introduction to the first of two volumes, Spengler proposed to trace the destiny of European-American culture—for Spengler, the only one on the planet that was fully realized—in the stages it had yet to go through. *The Decline of the West* is still considered an important expression of cultural pessimism. It ran through several editions and was one of the most influential works of cultural history in the 1920s, even if it also came in for hefty criticism. Thomas Mann, for example, initially praised

Spengler's work before ultimately rejecting it as "hostile to the future and fatalistic."

19. After achieving the unification of the German Reich in 1871, Reich Chancellor Otto von Bismarck tried to establish Germany as a "free mediator" and "honest broker." Bismarck recognized that the biggest threat to the Reich was a two-front war with France to the west and Russia to the east, and he sought to neutralize the danger with a complex system of alliances.

20. Franz Moraller (1903–1986) was a leading functionary within the Nazi propaganda apparatus. Beginning in 1942, he was the editor in chief of the *Strassburger Neueste Nachrichten,* the Nazi newspaper in Alsace.

21. For the Nazis, Germans collectively comprised an "ethnic popular community" (*Volksgemeinschaft*) to which Jews and political enemies had no access. The Nazis explicitly contrasted the idea of community with that of society, which had "un-German" connotations. In describing himself as an "ethnic comrade" (*Volksgenosse*), Müller-Hill is ironically appropriating a buzzword of Nazi propaganda that was supposed to remind individuals of their connection to the collective. Such terminology, of course, did at least as much to exclude unwanted others as to include group members.

22. It is unclear here why the date of November 9, 1943 should mark an ostensible turning point in the war. There were no significant military events on this day. November 9 was, however, very important in the National Socialist calendar since it was on that day in 1923 that Hitler attempted to overthrow the government of Munich in the so-called Beer Hall Putsch. The Führer always marked this occasion with "old comrades" from the "fighting years" of the party.

23. Müller-Hill refers here to Hitler's speech in Saarbrücken on October 9, 1938, only ten days after the signing of the Munich Agreement, in which he spoke of a "new world war," announced that "more energy" would be devoted to building the Siegfried Line, and proclaimed the "resurrection of a proud, strong, and free German Reich." See Max Domarus, *Hitler: Reden und Proklamationen 1932–1945,* vol. 1, part 2: *Triumph 1935–1938* (Munich: Bolchazy-Carducci, 1965).

24. Hungary initially sided with Nazi Germany and declared war on the Soviet Union, Britain, and the United States. But as of 1943, concerned by German defeat at Stalingrad, it tried to distance itself from Hitler and reach an agreement with Stalin. On March 19, 1944, Hitler ordered German troops to occupy Hungary. The events Müller-Hill refers to here—the siege of Budapest and the conquest of Hungary by the Red Army first took place in February 1945, somewhat later than he predicted.

25. Once it had become clear that Italian dictator Benito Mussolini had gotten in over his head with his Africa campaign, Hitler deployed German forces under the command of General Erwin Rommel. After some initial successes, they were gradually pushed back on the defensive. By March 1943, Hitler had to withdraw the so-called Desert Fox, who had been promoted to the rank of field marshal but who was ultimately unsuccessful. The man who relived him of his command, Major General Hans-Jürgen von Arnim, could do little more than raise the

white flag in May 1943. It is possible that the letter Müller-Hill refers to here was older since the passage cited suggests that fighting was still going on at that point.

26. Japan was the third major partner in the Axis but was an unreliable ally. Fear of the United States led the Japanese to reach an agreement with the Soviet Union on April 13, 1941, to the detriment of Nazi Germany.

27. *Das Reich* was a weekly cultural and political newspaper founded by Goebbels. It was targeted at people abroad and the intellectual bourgeoisie and was intended to mitigate the monotony of state-run press under National Socialism. Part of the basic idea of the paper was to publish exclusive material not available to other periodicals. Goebbels often wrote the editorials himself. The board of editors was made up of well-known journalists who had earlier worked for liberal and conservative newspapers. In 1944 the paper achieved a circulation of one million. It was published from May 26, 1940 to April 15, 1945.

28. The Allied invasion of the Atlantic coastline as part of Operation Overlord was to become a reality two months later. On June 6, 1944, Allied troops landed at Normandy, and in only a matter of hours it was clear that the invasion deserved the nickname D-Day. Within five weeks, the Allies were able to bring ashore more than 1.5 million men. Müller-Hill's fears that an invasion would decide the war were thus entirely justified.

29. The Seven Years' War (1756–1763) was both a battle between Prussia and Austria for Silesia and a struggle between the European powers for overseas predominance, regarded by people at the time as the first-ever world war. Prussia was faced with near-certain defeat when the empress Elizabeth of Russia—the bitterest enemy of Prussian king Frederick II (Frederick the Great)—suddenly died in Saint Petersburg on January 5, 1762. She was succeeded by the emperor Peter III, an admirer of Frederick, who made peace and subsequently concluded an alliance with Prussia. Conveniently ignoring the fact that Peter III was assassinated shortly thereafter and the Russian-Prussian alliance canceled, Hitler and his lackeys drew parallels with this series of events as historical evidence that changes within the enemy leadership could dramatically alter the outcome of war.

30. *Pimpfe* was the name for members of the Deutsches Jungvolk (German Youth), a subdivision of the Hitler Youth for boys aged 10 to 14. The altered song text Müller-Hill refers to plays on the similarity between the words *gehören* (belong to) and *hören* (listen to). The song in question was entitled "Es zittern die morschen Knochen" (The Old Bones Are Quaking) and was written, as were many Hitler Youth songs, by the composer Hans Baumann. There is little other evidence of the song text being altered in the way Müller-Hill describes.

31. Founded in 1920, the Sturmabteilung (Storm Division) was the Nazis' party militia. After the heads of the organization were murdered in the Night of the Long Knives on June 30, 1934, the SA's membership began to decline and the group was transformed into an ideologically secure, permanently mobilized force for the regime. During World War II, the SA was involved in premilitary training and helped build up the

Volkssturm, the popular militia raised in Hitler's last-ditch effort to achieve victory. In its early days, the SA's campaign of brutally terrorizing people on the streets created a sense of permanent threat. The later marches and parades, of which Müller-Hill writes here, were rituals enacting the "Führer cult."

32. *Der Alemanne* was the name of a daily newspaper in Freiburg published by the Nazis. The periodical defined itself as an "advocate for National Socialist Upper Baden." The first edition appeared in November 1931 and the paper was banned after the collapse of the Nazi system in 1945. The original quote from Goethe reads "Stay a while, you are so beautiful" and comes from the bargain Faust makes with Mephistopheles in *Faust,* Part 1.

33. Odessa was the most important Black Sea port in the Ukraine. Its loss meant that Germany was no longer able to wage war in the Black Sea.

34. Shortly after coming to power, the National Socialists criminalized critical statements about the regime. On March 21, 1933, the government issued the "Ordinance of the Reich President for Defense against Perfidious Attacks on the Government of National Renewal," which made even private remarks eligible for criminal prosecution. According to paragraph 3 of that ordinance, it was a punishable offense for someone to make "an untrue or crassly distorted assertion," the content of which aimed at damaging the reputation of the government and its main parties. A year later, after Nazi rule had been consolidated, the ordinance was superseded by the "Law against Perfidious Attacks on the State and Party and for the Protection of Party Uniforms" of December 20, 1934. Its paragraph 2 criminalized "private, malicious utterances . . . insofar as the person making them should have known that they could become public." To speed up the punishment of those accused of making "perfidious" remarks, special political courts were established to prosecute them. In 1933, these encompassed 26 criminal divisions. By 1942, that number had nearly tripled to 74. Defendants enjoyed very few of the normal rights in of such courts, whose verdicts could only be appealed before the Reichsgericht, Germany's supreme court.

35. As of 1939, Colonel General Friedrich Fromm (1888–1945) was made commander of the Replacement Army, which made him part of the military high command. He was privy to the plans for the anti-Hitler coup on July 20, 1944, but refused to take sides. His attempt to save his own skin by having Claus Schenk von Stauffenberg and members of the putsch executed failed. He was later arrested and executed for "cowardice" in March 1945.

36. The reference is apparently to the novel *The Case of Sergeant Grischa* by Arnold Zweig. It was translated into English and adapted into a film in 1930.

37. The Battle of Stalingrad was probably the most significant and decisive military defeat suffered by Hitler in the war he had started. Following weeks of fighting, first for victory, then for sheer survival, General Friedrich Paulus capitulated on January 31, 1943, almost ten years to the day after Hitler assumed power as Reich Chancellor. Psychologically, Stalingrad was also a major caesura, as Müller-Hill's diary entry makes clear.

The Hitler greeting—the raising of the extended right arm accompanied by the words "Heil Hitler!"—was derived from the fascist greeting of Mussolini. In many social situations, the use of the Hitler greeting or lack thereof signaled an individual's level of identification with the Nazi Party. It was a more reliable index than even party membership. As the end of the war approached and the Nazis' command over society began to slip for many Germans, the Hitler greeting was used less and less. The sentence was crossed out in the original diary.

38. "*Germany Calling*" was the German foreign radio service initiated by Goebbels. It broadcast a mix of news and music in 30 languages and was aimed particularly at listeners in Britain and the United States. The propaganda programs attracted attention by offering POWs the chance to send greetings to their loved ones back home. Many POWs made use of this opportunity, especially as their names were announced in advance so that relatives and friends would know when to tune in.

39. In the context of preparing for World War II and in a radical deviation from his previous, anti-Soviet foreign policy, Hitler ordered his Foreign Minister Joachim von Ribbentrop to negotiate a nonaggression pact with the Soviet Union. It was concluded on August 23, 1939, and was to last ten years. The pact allowed Hitler to attack Poland without becoming immediately embroiled in a two-front war. Also known as the Hitler-Stalin Pact, the agreement divided Poland's territory between the German Reich and the Soviet Union and defined each empire's sphere of influence. Subsequent economic treaties supplemented the pact, which became immediately null and void when Germany attacked the Soviet Union on June 22, 1941.

40. The reference is to the *Strassburger Neueste Nachrichten*, which reported on the bombardment of Strasbourg. Müller-Hill cut out the article cited and pasted it into his diary.

41. French for "Time will tell."

42. Albert Leo Schlageter, an early Nazi activist and member of the paramilitary Freikorps, was sentenced to death by a French military court during the occupation of the Ruhr Valley in 1923 and was honored as a martyr by nationalist groups during the Weimar Republic.

43. The author Daniele Varè (1880–1956) was an Italian novelist who drew heavily on his decades of experience as a diplomat in Vienna, Beijing, Geneva, Luxembourg, and London.

44. The Central Powers were Germany, the Austro-Hungarian Empire, the Ottoman Empire, and Bulgaria. Although allied with Germany and Austria-Hungary, Italy refused to get involved in World War I, and Mussolini initially sided with the Western Allies.

45. In October 1935, Mussolini attacked the East African empire of Abyssinia (today's Ethiopia) in an attempt to seize it as a colony. This act attracted enormous international criticism, which led Hitler to pursue the chance to draw closer to the Duce and recommend Germany as a partner. Secretly, though, Hitler was playing both sides of the game. He supplied Italian industry with coal and steel while sending arms to Ethiopia in the hope that a protracted conflict would tie Mussolini to him more closely. Hitler's calculations ultimately paid off. In May 1936 Mussolini won the war in Abyssinia and formed the Axis with Hitler.

46. In a referendum of March 1921 mandated by article 88 of the Treaty of Versailles, almost 60 percent of Upper Silesians voted to remain part of the German Reich. Polish paramilitaries, supported by French occupation troops, then tried to force the region to join Poland. With permission from Britain, to which Müller-Hill refers here, German paramilitaries mobilized as well. In October 1921 the Allies decided to partition Upper Silesia. Germany received the larger, mainly agricultural and thus economically less significant, section. The Upper Silesian industrial belt was ceded to Poland. The cessation of parts of Upper Silesia called forth national outrage across the political spectrum in Germany.

47. Current research, however, suggests that Reich Chancellor Heinrich Brüning was also trying to use the National Socialist movement to achieve his foreign-policy ends. Nonetheless, Müller-Hill sees quite correctly that any Allied compromise with the Weimar government would probably have cost Hitler support.

48. Ever since being put in charge of the Reich's Four Year Plan in 1936, Hermann Göring was considered the "economic dictator" of the Third Reich. With the beginning of Germany's campaign against Russia, Göring was also charged with economically exploiting occupied countries. But Göring's star declined dramatically with both the German public and with Hitler himself when the Luftwaffe, of which he was also in charge, disappointed expectations, most prominent in Germany's defeat in the Battle of Britain in 1940–41.

49. The reference is to Reich Armament Minister Albert Speer's order to work overtime in order to increase production of fighter planes.

50. Dr. G. refers to Goebbels.

51. On March 31, 1944, Field Marshal General Erich von Manstein (1887–1973) was relieved of his command after disagreements with Hitler. He was the author of the Manstein Plan, which resulted in Allied defeat and the evacuation of Dunkirk in 1940, which is what Müller-Hill presumably refers to here. In the Russian campaign, he was responsible for the conquest of Crimea. During the Battle of Stalingrad, he commanded Army Group Don, later Army Group South. He was credited with saving the German southern front in Russia from absolute destruction. In 1945, Manstein was captured and sentenced to twelve years imprisonment, of which he was only required to serve a small part because of poor health. He was released in 1953, after which he wrote his memoirs and advised West Germany on the establishment of the Bundeswehr.

52. Walter Model (1891–1945), considered by Hitler to be someone who had demonstrated his National Socialist credentials on both the western and eastern fronts, was promoted to field marshall general and supreme commander of Army Group North Ukraine. In the wake of the failed assassination attempt of July 20, 1944, he would prove to be one of the military leaders most loyal to the Führer, insisting that Germany fight for ultimate victory to the very end of World War II. Shortly before the end of the war, he avoided being called to account for his actions by committing suicide.

53. In his 1943 New Year's address, a few weeks before German troops finally capitulated at Stalingrad, Hitler stated: "If in the past year the

German Wehrmacht and the nations allied with us have succeeded in pushing the Bolshevik line that particularly threatens Europe even further back, then the men and women of the German home front, town and country, have also achieved something unique under the most difficult of circumstances." See Max Domarus, *Hitler, Reden und Proklamationen 1932–1945*, vol. 2, part 2: *Untergang 1941–1945* (Munich: Bolchazy-Carducci, 1965).

54. The reference is probably to Hans Schwarz van Berk, a fanatic Nazi who wrote under the pseudonym Hans Hansen and published numerous articles in *Das Reich* encouraging Germans to hold out against defeat.

55. On January 22, 1944, Allied troops landed at Nettuno on the Tyrrhenian Sea in Italy. The Wehrmacht tried in vain to prevent them from advancing on Rome.

56. Nazi propaganda portrayed the "boycott" of Jewish-owned stores, doctors, and lawyers, or those thought to be owned by Jews, of April 1, 1933, as a response to demands for anti-German boycotts and "terrible propaganda" from abroad. (In reality, this was more of a state-sanctioned, massive blockade of Jews' participation in the economy than a true boycott by customers, patients, clients, and consumers.) With this action, the regime demonstrated that it intended to hold Jews in Germany responsible for foreign criticism of the Nazi regime. The April boycott marked the beginning of what Müller-Hill calls the "miserable," pre-Holocaust policies toward Jews, which led to the anti-Semitic violence of 1935, the gradual destruction of Jews' economic existence, and the Night of Broken Glass on November 9, 1938.

57. The use of the phrase "party comrades" to refer to members of the National Socialist German Workers Party originally distinguished them from members of the Socialist and Communists Parties, who simply called themselves "comrades." On January 1, 1935, official Nazi Party statistics put the number of members at 2.5 million, two-thirds of whom only joined after the Nazis had assumed power on January 30, 1933. In 1945, the Nazi Party had 8.5 million members.

58. In November 1918, four years after the outbreak of hostilities in World War I, the German Reich capitulated. In the immediate wake of their defeat, few Germans would have described the situation as "idyllic." The abdication of Kaiser Wilhelm II, the November Revolution, the revanchist Treaty of Versailles, and the massive reparations demanded by the Allies left no doubt that Germans would pay dearly for the war.

59. Heinrich Himmer (1900–1945) was one of Hitler's closest intimates. As of June 1936, as the head of the SS and the German police, he was in charge of the entire Nazi apparatus for terrorizing and repressing Germany's citizenry. In 1939 he became Reich Commissioner for the Consolidation of German Ethnicity. In 1943 he was made German Minister of the Interior, and in 1944 Hitler assigned him command over the Replacement Army. Himmler avoided responsibility for countless acts of terror and murder by committing suicide as a British POW in 1945.

60. At the start of June 1944, the Wehrmacht abandoned Rome without a fight to the Allies. By this point, Mussolini was little more than a

puppet, dependent on Hitler's favor, at the head of the so-called Italian Social Republic.

61. To avoid acknowledging that Germany had been defeated military in World War I, right-wing nationalists concocted and spread the myth that Germany had not been bested on the field of battle. "The German army was stabbed in the back," Paul von Hindenburg, the former supreme commander of German forces and later Reich president, told a parliamentary committee in 1919. As evidence for this claim, advocates of what is commonly known as the stab-in-the-back legend cited the November Revolution and the armistice. The myth of internal betrayal was a crucial element in German society's repression and denial of military defeat.

62. Geheime Staatspolizei (Secret State Police), or Gestapo, was the central organ with which the Nazi regime terrorized and repressed its own citizenry. It evolved from the Prussian Political Police. Led by Reinhard Heydrich, the Gestapo's job was to identify and apprehend political adversaries and those excluded from the National Socialist "ethnic community." The Gestapo often arrested people on no legal grounds whatsoever. The organization's many spies created an atmosphere of latent threat and surveillance. However, the myth of the Gestapo as an all-knowing government police force far exceeded the organization's actual surveillance capabilities. Heydrich was assassinated in 1942, and his place was taken by Ernst Kaltenbrunner.

The Schutzstaffeln (Protective Squadrons), or SS, were initially "elite" formations within the Nazi Party with the highest standards for membership. In early 1929, Heinrich Himmler became the *Reichsführer* or leader of the organization and transformed it into a party police force and a militarized unit to execute the Führer's will. The most notorious sections were the bodyguards "Adolf Hitler," the Totenkopfverbände (Death's Head Units), the Waffen-SS, and the concentration camp guards.

63. The reference is to Goebbels's speech in Nuremberg at the mass rally during the regional Nazi Party day on June 4, 1944. In it, Goebbels declared: "We can only say that in the west we are ready. And if the enemy comes, we'll teach him a lesson. Of course we cannot publicize the details of how we have gotten ready and what we've prepared for . . . I can only say [our miracle weapon] will be used when it has the greatest chance of success! . . . We secretly hope that when retribution comes, it will be decisive in the war. That is what we hope." See *Goebbels-Reden*, vol. 2: *1939–1945*, edited by Helmut Heiber (Düsseldorf: Droste, 1972), 335. The speech was published by various newspapers across the Reich and was probably also broadcast on radio after the Normandy invasion.

64. The reference is to the Dieppe Raid of August 19, 1942. In it, some 6,000 largely Canadian infantrymen, supported by the British Navy and Royal Air Force, launched an attack of the German occupied port of Dieppe in France. The raid was quickly repelled.

65. The captain was also a so-called IC, the third-highest ranking staff officer in the Prussian army and the Wehrmacht, who was responsible for evaluating the enemy's situation and for intelligence gathering.

66. The reference is to Goethe's two-volume bildungsroman *Wilhelm Meister.*

67. Ascona is a town in Italian-speaking Switzerland. At this late point in World War II, it was unusual for Germans to be able to travel to Switzerland.

68. The Wehrmacht conquered the Byelorussian town of Vitebsk on July 10, 1941.

69. In December 1943, Dwight D. Eisenhower was made the Supreme Allied Commander in Europe. After the end of the war, he served as the commander in chief of American occupation forces in Germany and was then appointed army chief of staff. He was the 34th president of the United States (1953–1961).

70. The battle of Cherbourg from June 6 to June 30, 1944, was a crucial event in World War II because it gave the Allies a deep-water port in which to land troops and matériel.

71. Joachim von Ribbentrop (1893–1946) succeeded Baron Konstantin von Neurath as Hitler's foreign minister in February 1938, but he never attained a position of true political influence. Hitler used him as something of a special envoy, for instance, to prepare for the Hitler-Stalin Pact in August 1939. Ribbentrop ordered the Foreign Ministry to cooperate fully in the persecution of Jews. He was captured in 1945 and found guilty of major war crimes at the Nuremberg Trials. He was executed on October 15, 1946. The jibe "champagne-bearing politician" refers to the fact that Ribbentrop's wife was the daughter of a major German sparkling-wine manufacturer.

72. The term Müller-Hill uses is *Götterdämmerung* (Twilight of the Gods), the title of the fourth part of Richard Wagner's "*Ring*" cycle. Not least because of his enthusiasm for Germanic myths, Wagner was Hitler's favorite composer and was regarded as something of an unofficial German national artist.

73. The term "*levée en masse*" stems from the mass-mobilization of male civilians in August 1793 to help the army of Revolutionary France, which was at war with various European enemies. Thanks to a law passed by the National Convention and the Committee of Public Safety, all unmarried men between the ages of 18 and 25 were drafted. The ranks of the French quickly swelled to a million men, and this helped France achieve victory. The *levée en masse* later served as a model for other European states introducing conscription.

74. As of February 1938, Wilhelm Keitel (1882–1946) was the head of the Wehrmacht Supreme Command and a member of the regime's uppermost military leadership, which made him complicit in a number of war crimes. In 1940 Keitel, whose fealty to Hitler earned him the nickname "Lackey," was promoted to the rank of field marshal. He was at the center of Nazi's Germany biggest military triumph and most catastrophic defeat. On June 22, 1940, he accepted France's capitulation in Compiègne and on May 8, 1945, he signed Germany's unconditional surrender in Karlshorst near Berlin. In 1946 he was sentenced to death by hanging at the Nuremberg Trials. He was executed in October 1946.

75. The preceding sentence would be more logical if it read "responsible people."

76. The attempted assassination of Hitler on June 20, 1944, was one of the most important acts of German resistance to Hitler. A group of conspirators lead by Count Claus Schenk von Stauffenberg (1907–1944) hatched a plot to place a bomb in Hitler's "Wolf's Lair" headquarters in East Prussia. Unfortunately, the group lacked supporters, meaning that Stauffenberg was responsible both for placing the bomb and organizing what was supposed to be the ensuing coup d'état. Hitler was only slightly injured in the explosion and the attempted coup quickly failed. The conspirators were subsequently executed.

77. "The butchery of 1934" refers to Hitler's purging of SA leader Ernst Röhm and members of the conservative elite on June 30, 1934, under the pretense of stopping an imminent "counterrevolution." The purge was carried out by the SS with help from the Wehrmacht and became known as the Night of the Long Knives. As a result, the SA lost status and the Wehrmacht was made complicit in the criminal policies of the government. Thus, June 30, 1934, marked an important stage in the consolidation of the regime's power. Müller-Hill's reference to this event as "butchery" ten years after the fact shows how present it remained in the minds of people at the time.

78. As previously discussed, Fromm knew of the coup plans but refused to get involved, so Müller-Hill's remark about him disappearing is entirely apt.

79. Turkey remained neutral through most of World War II, entering the conflict on the side of the Allies as a largely symbolic gesture on February 23, 1945.

80. Risto Ryti (1889–1956) was president of Finland from 1940 to 1944. In June 1944, he negotiated the Ryti-Ribbentrop Agreement, in which Germany agreed to provide Finland with grain and weapons for its war against the Soviet Union. After Finland successfully repelled the Soviet offensive, Ryti stepped down, officially for health reasons. On August 4, 1944, his successor Carl Gustaf Emil Mannerheim (1867–1951) was elected. He would remain Finnish president until 1946. Under his leadership and over German opposition, he concluded a truce with the Soviet Union.

81. Roland Freisler (1898–1945) joined the Hitler regime as a judicial state secretary in 1933 and had enormous influence over Nazi legal policies as the editor of the *Zeitschrift der Akademie für Deutsches Recht*. In 1942 he became head of the notorious People's Court. Defendants who came up before him had little chance. Ninety percent of his verdicts were death sentences or sentences of life imprisonment. Freisler was known for humiliating defendants, often shouting at the top of his lungs during trials—a habit that was criticized even among the Nazi leadership. He was killed in the cellar of the People's Court during an air raid in February 1945.

82. Lieutenant General Paul von Hase (1885–1944), one of Stauffenberg's coconspirators.

83. Alfred Rosenberg (1893–1946) was the self-styled chief ideologist of the Nazi party. His main work was *Der Mythus des 20. Jahrhunderts* (English translation: *The Myth of the Twentieth Century*), which was published in 1930. In 1934 Hitler named him the "Führer's Commissioner for the Surveillance of the Entire Spiritual and Ideological

Education of the NSDAP." Rosenberg advocated the destruction of the Christian Church, but Hitler deemed that inopportune in the short term. As of 1941, Rosenberg also held the title of "Reich Minister for the Occupied Eastern Territories." He was sentenced to death and executed in Nuremberg in October 1946.

84. Men in Nazi Germany were exempted from military service if they possessed special skills or performed especially important civilian functions.

85. In October 1939 Colonel General Johannes Blaskowitz (1883–1948) was the German supreme commander east, but was relieved of his command after writing memoranda condemning the brutality of SS units. In May 1944 he was put in charge of Army Group G, a relatively small force responsible for defending southern France from the Allied invasion. After the war, in the interest of providing civilians with the necessities of life, he worked together with the Allies. He committed suicide in 1948 when the Allies wanted to put him on trial for war crimes.

86. Épinal was the regional capital of Lorraine.

87. This passage may refer to the Siegfried Line, the defensive fortifications partially completed in 1938–39 by the Organisation Todt and the Reich Labor Service. While the line did have some deterrent effect on the Allies in 1939–40, it proved of little use in 1944–45.

88. Arminius, the chieftain of the Germanic Cherusci, dramatically defeated the Roman army under Varus in the Battle of the Teutoburg Forest in September of the year 9 A.D. This triumph made him the most famous figure in early Germanic history. Tacitus called him "Germania's liberator."

89. The philosopher and politician Michel de Montaigne (1533–92) was a court officer before a generous inheritance allowed him to withdraw into private life. A trip intended to help him overcome a kidney condition took him from Paris to Germany and finally to Rome. He kept a diary during his journey.

90. Bose Indians were leaders of the movement for Indian independence from Britain. In 1944 they founded an "Indian legion," which was put under the command of the Waffen-SS.

91. Günther von Kluge (1882–1944) was a general staff officer in World War I who was named field marshal general in July 1940. He commanded major army units in Germany's campaigns against Poland, France, and the Soviet Union. In July 1944, he was given supreme command of the Army West and a short time later over Army Group B. He nonetheless came under suspicion of disloyalty and was relieved of his posts. On August 19, 1944, he committed suicide. A short time earlier, he had written a farewell letter to Hitler, protesting his loyalty but calling for an end to the war.

92. The V-3 was ostensibly a super-cannon. In soldier's slang, V-3 also referred to the *Volkssturm,* the popular militia that was only sporadically equipped with weapons and that had no real effect on the course of the war.

93. In a speech to the Reichstag on December 6, 1897, Bernhard von Bülow, state secretary in the Foreign Ministry and later Reich chancellor, said: "We don't want to leave anyone in our shadow, but we

demand our place in the sun." This expression is often mistakenly attributed to Kaiser Wilhelm II and is taken as a pithy summary of his colonial ambitions.

94. Müller-Hill is playing upon Kaiser Wilhelm II's "free hand" foreign policy, which was regarded as megalomaniac and which aimed at establishing the German Reich as a world power. William's high-handed behavior increasingly isolated Germany and represented a break with the policies of Bismarck, who emphasized the need for Germany to maintain balanced alliances.

95. The *Anschluss,* the unification of Austria with Germany, was one of Hitler's biggest propaganda coups. Most of Austria cheered the German "Führer and Reich Chancellor," as he announced the "world-historical" news of the entry of his homeland into the German Reich. Müller-Hill's remark about the country soon being "healed" is perhaps meant to indicate that Austrians had been deceived about what membership in the Reich actually entailed. After 1945, most Austrians preferred to forget how enthusiastically they had celebrated Hitler and instead developed the national myth that their country had been Hitler's first "victim."

96. *Triarii* were experienced, heavily armed soldiers in ancient Rome.

97. Dysentery is a disease contracted through the digestive system and is often encouraged by weakened immune systems and poor public hygiene.

98. The reference is to German propaganda claims that, wherever Nazi rule encountered resistance, Bolsheviks, Jews, or, even better, "Jewish Bolshevists" were to blame.

99. Although hyperinflation in post-1918 Germany had catastrophic effects on many people and scorched itself onto the collective memories of that and following generations, industry and state finances profited from the devaluation of German currency. The Reich Central Bank was able to offer industry short-term lines of credit since there was far more money in circulation, and many companies used the opportunity to expand. The industrial magnate Hugo Stinnes, for instance, built up a huge economic empire by racking up larger and larger debts since those debts later became worthless. Likewise the state profited since its immense war debts, once amounting to hundreds of billions of reichsmarks, were worth only pennies after the currency revaluation of November 1923.

100. The officer was a recipient of Knight's Cross with Oak Leaves, Swords, and Diamonds, one of highest decorations in the Third Reich.

101. It is unclear to which composer named Kaufmann Müller-Hill is referring here. The director would seem to be Charles Münch, who was not in fact killed in the aerial bomboardment, but went on to have a long postwar career, conducting the Boston Symphony Orchestra among others.

102. As of April 1944, Herbert Backe (1896–1944) was the head of the Ministry of Food and Agriculture.

103. The German-Swiss Heinrich Anacker (1901–1971), a Nazi party member since 1924, worked as a propaganda author and held a seat as a culture senator in the cultural council of Reich Writers' Chamber. With the onset of World War II, Anacker renounced his Swiss

citizenship and volunteered as a war correspondent and soldier for Hitler's regime.

104. Sparta was an ancient Greek city synonymous with strict, disciplined asceticism. Capua was the most powerful and wealthiest city in the Campania region of ancient southern Italy. The luxurious life there supposedly robbed the Punic army of strength and battle readiness during the Second Punic War.

105. Müller-Hill seems to mean the night before, November 21, 1944.

106. In mid-March 1918, roughly three weeks after the Treaty of Brest-Litovsk, which ended hostilities between Germany and Russia in World War I, the German Supreme Army Command in western Europe launched an all-or-nothing offensive. Code-named "Michael," it was intended to convince the Western Allies to sue for peace, and at first it seemed promising. German troops succeeded in breaking through English lines over a stretch of 80 kilometers and pressing 60 kilometers onward. But they failed in their aim of separating French and English troops. German forces managed to advance all the way to the Marne by the end of May 1918, but that brought no strategic advantage. The temporary triumph had come at too high a price. The Supreme Army Command had been too ambitious and had to accept that defeat was inevitable.

107. John Galsworthy, *Caravan: The Assembled Tales* (London: William Heinemann, 1925). Galsworthy (1867–1933) was an English writer and dramatist best known for *The Forsyte Saga*. He won the Nobel Prize for literature in 1932.

108. The Nazi name for the central region of occupied Poland.

109. The reference is to Hans Fritzsche (April 21, 1900–September 27, 1953), the Ministerial Director of the Propaganda Ministry, whose responsibilities included radio broadcasts. He was tried at Nuremberg and became one of only three defendants to be acquitted there.

110. The National Socialist Welfare, or NSV, was an organization founded by a decree by Hitler on May 3, 1933. It was responsible for taking care of "needy ethnic comrades" deemed worthy of support in political, racial, and genetic terms. The NSV aimed to produce a healthy "collective ethnic body." The organization's work thus focused on the capability of the community and not on the material or social misery of individuals. Moreover, the NSV served the propaganda needs of a regime that wanted to prove it was instituting "socialism of deeds." In 1938 the NSV had 11 million members and one million volunteer workers. They were chiefly concerned with disease prevention, but they also maintained train station missions, an "assistance society for German graphic arts" and a food relief organization. In August 1944 Hitler proclaimed that the NSV was a "bearer and representative of popular hygiene." In so doing, he reaffirmed the increasing convergence of party and state interests in the NSV.

111. Müller-Hill is possibly playing upon a statement Hitler made on September 30, 1939, when inaugurating the Winter Relief Organization: "The Jews, those in Germany as well, once laughed at my prophecies. I don't know whether they're still laughing today or whether their laughter has stuck in their throats. But I can assure you: their laughter

everywhere will stick in their throats." See Domarus, *Hitler, Reden und Proklamationen, 1932–1945,* vol. 2, part 2: *Untergang 1941–1945.*

112. The word "cratoplutes" originated in a joke during the Third Reich that ironically played upon the hostility of Nazi propaganda toward Anglo-American "plutocracy." The joke ran: whereas plutocrats acquired power with money, Nazi cratoplutes did the exact opposite. The joke drew attention to widespread corruption and the privileges enjoyed by party bigwigs under National Socialism.

113. In retrospect, the majority of the Third Reich leadership hardly faced death with their heads held high. The majority of political and military elites committed suicide and tried to go underground. According to historian Ludolf Herbst, the way they dealt with the downfall of Third Reich was evidence of the Nazi elites' "mediocrity of intellect and character."

114. November 9, 1938, was the so-called Night of Broken Glass, the propagandistic, state-orchestrated pogrom against German Jews that was intended to look like a spontaneous outbreak of popular anti-Semitic hostility. Müller-Hill refers with astonishing openness here to the mass shootings of Jews behind the front in occupied territories as well as the industrial-style genocide of Jews who were gassed to death in the concentration camps of eastern Europe.

115. Herbert Norkus (1916–1932) was a Hitler Youth who was killed in 1932 at the age of 15 in an altercation with Communists. In National Socialism, he was considered a "role model for the battling heroism of the Hitler Youth" and was lionized and instrumentalized by party propaganda as a "martyr for the movement." The day after his death, the Nazi newspaper *Der Angriff* (The Attack) ran the headline: "How Hitler Youth Herbert Norkus was massacred by Red murderers." Norkus' short life served as the inspiration for the propagandistic novel and film "*Hitler Youth Quex*" as well as for many Hitler Youth songs. During the Third Reich, a sailboat, an orphanage, and numerous schools, streets, and town squares were named after him.

116. Paul Reynaud (1878–1966) became French prime minister in March 1940. A bourgeois centrist, he resisted French defeat by Nazi Germany. He rejected the idea of reaching an understanding with Hitler and he resigned when he saw that his plan to continue the fight from France's colonies couldn't be realized. He was arrested by his deputy and successor, Marshal Philippe Pétain. After being deported to the German Reich in 1942, he was incarcerated. After the end of the war, he was a leading advocate of German-French reconciliation and European unity.

Pétain (1856–1951) was a French national hero for his role in the defense of Verdun in World War I. As deputy prime minister in Reynaud's government, he advocated making peace with Nazi Germany. Having been promoted to prime minister after Reynaud's resignation, he concluded armistices with Germany and Italy. In the Vichy system, Pétain was French "head of state." He refused offers to become a junior partner to Hitler in ruling over Europe. After the war, Pétain was sentenced to death for high treason and betrayal of his country. He was pardoned and served a life sentence in a citadel on the Île d'Yeu.

117. This sentence and the preceding one were crossed out in Müller-Hill's diary.

118. The saying "my country right or wrong" in fact originated in the United States and is usually attributed to either naval officer Stephen Decatur or statesman Carl Schurz.

119. Latin saying: "What is permitted to Jupiter is not permitted to an ox." The saying is used to draw attention to unequal starting points and privileges.

120. Drumhead courts-martial held speedy trials, without any of the usual legal procedure, and their verdicts were carried out on the spot. They had been tried out in occupied Poland for the purpose of immediately liquidating resistance fighters. An edict of November 1, 1939, had deemed drumhead courts permissible within the Wehrmacht. In June 1943 the Reich War Court was expanded to include a central drumhead court for political offenses. On February 1945 an edict was issued entitled "Formation of Generally Responsible Courts-Martial," consisting of judge, a party functionary, and an officer. So-called "flying" courts-martial were particularly feared toward the end of the war. Thousands of critics of the Nazi regime are thought to have been sentenced to death by such courts.

121. This sentence is crossed out in the original diary.

122. The town of Wolfurt meant here is located near Lake Constance in what is today Austria.

YOU MAY ALSO LIKE ...

Mr. Flesh Pool
– by Richard Rose

The Tragedy of Liberation: A History of
Frank Dikötter

... by Fritz Stein

Show
by Oliver Pötzsch

other retailers or sellers from which they are purchased, retailer or seller from which they are purchased, pursuant to such retailer's or seller's return policy. Magazines, newspapers, eBooks, digital downloads, and used books are not returnable or exchangeable. Defective NOOKs may be exchanged at the store in accordance with the applicable warranty.

Returns or exchanges will not be permitted (i) after 14 days or without receipt or (ii) for product not carried by Barnes & Noble or Barnes & Noble.com.

Policy on receipt may appear in two sections.

Return Policy

With a sales receipt or Barnes & Noble.com packing slip, a full refund in the original form of payment will be issued from any Barnes & Noble Booksellers store for returns of undamaged NOOKs, new and unread books, and unopened and undamaged music CDs, DVDs, and audio books made within 14 days of purchase from a Barnes & Noble Booksellers store or Barnes & Noble.com with the below exceptions: